JAZZ BAND PIANIST
BASIC SKILLS FOR THE JAZZ BAND PIANIST

Recording Personnel: The Western Michigan University Advanced Jazz Ensemble: Curtis James, trumpet; Dominic Carioti, saxophone; Denis Shebukhov, bass; Steven Perry, drums; Jeremy Siskind, piano, producer; Nich Mueller, assistant producer; Brian Heany, engineer; John Campos, engineer.

To access audio visit:
www.halleonard.com/mylibrary

Enter Code
2505-1518-6283-8088

ISBN 978-1-4768-0595-5

HAL•LEONARD® CORPORATION

7777 W. BLUEMOUND RD. P.O. BOX 13819 MILWAUKEE, WI 53213

In Australia Contact:
Hal Leonard Australia Pty. Ltd.
4 Lentara Court
Cheltenham, Victoria, 3192 Australia
Email: ausadmin@halleonard.com.au

Visit Hal Leonard Online at
www.halleonard.com

TABLE OF CONTENTS

Dedicated with gratitude to those who have taught me how to play jazz over the years: Linda Martinez, Tamir Hendleman, Tony Caramia, Harold Danko, and Fred Hersch.

INTRODUCTION

Playing piano in a jazz band is one of the most difficult jobs in music. A jazz band pianist instantaneously translates chord symbols into sophisticated voicings, spontaneously creating accompaniments to support complex arrangements and a variety of soloists. This book gradually guides a pianist from learning basic jazz harmonies to translating chord symbols and rhythmic notation with ease.

The piano part you'll receive for a jazz band piece typically takes one of two approaches:

1) Mostly chord symbols and diagonal slashes, with very few actual notes:

2) Quickly-changing chords written out with chord symbols above the staff:

These two approaches actually express the same thing. The chord symbols and slashes of the first example provide directions for the pianist. The chords written out in the second example represent *one possible realization* of those directions.

When reading the latter, you *could* ignore the chord symbols and play the chords of the example as written. However, you'd be doing yourself a major disservice because:

1. When you receive a part without written notes, you'll have no practice reading the chord symbols.

2. Chord symbols are a shorthand notation to make reading chords easier and quicker. Once you understand them, they're much simpler to read than the written-out chords.

3. Most importantly, reading the chord symbols allows for improvisation. **Improvisation** is the art of spontaneous creation. In jazz, this includes interacting with fellow musicians, making decisions specific to each musical moment, and experiencing uninhibited self-expression.

Please consider this book an introduction to the art of playing in a jazz band; it covers the most essential portion of what a jazz pianist needs to know. A teacher, other books, and recordings (a brief list can be found in the appendix on p. 152) can serve as further guides once you've mastered these pages.

If being a jazz pianist is one of the hardest roles in music, it's also one of the most rewarding. If you master the information in this book, you'll be prepared to play in a jazz band and experience first-hand the thrill of America's great art form.

HOW TO USE THIS BOOK

ORGANIZATION

Most chapters are divided into three sections:

1. Instructional text that introduces a new concept

2. "To the Shed" – written exercises that reinforce your knowledge of the material; answers are found in the index

3. Pieces to practice that create muscle memory and put the new concepts into action

AUDIO

Since it will be helpful to hear the melody and the bass, it's very important that you practice with the provided play-along audio. Two tracks are provided for each piece – one without piano, designed for play-along, and one with piano, designed for reference.

Each piece has an "unrealized" version – music with no notes written for the piano; and a "realized" version – an "answer key" with fully written-out voicings. For practice purposes, feel free to read through the realized version first to get the chords "under your fingers"; then attempt to read only the unrealized version, continuing to use the realized version for reference.

PIANO PART

Each piece includes a piano part similar to what you might be given in a jazz band and a written melody for reference only – *not* for you to play. In a jazz band, the pianist is generally not playing the melody. You should focus on translating the chord symbols and (in the later chapters) forming voicings.

Happy practicing!
–Jeremy Siskind

CHAPTER 1
RHYTHM BASICS

When you look at a piece of jazz music for the first time, you might be surprised that you're expected to play music with no notes. The chord symbols above the staff indicate what notes to play. Most of this book is dedicated to deciphering these symbols. The rhythms you choose, however, are equally important.

COMPING

Choosing your own rhythm for chords is called **comping**. This word abbreviates either "accompanying" or "complementing", depending who you ask. The indication that you should *comp* is fat diagonal slashes:

Each slash represents one beat during which the pianist freely interprets the most recent chord symbol. The Cm7 and F7 chords in the above example last for four beats while the B♭maj7 lasts for eight.*

Sometimes chords change in the middle of a measure. To indicate such a change, the new symbol is placed over the slash representing the beat on which the chord changes. In the example below, the G7 starts on beat 4.

When reading slashes, any rhythm is hypothetically acceptable. When you see:

....you could play:

...or:

*Don't worry about the chord symbols for now, these will be explained in the chapters ahead!

....or even:

The best rhythm to play depends on the style. You should choose different rhythmic patterns for a rock beat, an R&B groove, or a jazz setting. So what comping rhythms are the best for jazz bands? We'll focus on two of the most common jazz rhythms:

THE CHARLESTON

The *Charleston* is a dance that was popular in the 1920's. Its moves are coordinated with a specific rhythm – a downbeat plus an upbeat anticipating the third beat:

This rhythm is well suited for jazz because it combines the stability of a downbeat with the rhythmic excitement of **syncopation**, that is, rhythm highlighting offbeats.

In the *Charleston* rhythm, the second chord of the measure acts as an **anticipation** of the third beat – *not* a delay of the second. A chord on the third beat must be played on the "and of two", anticipating the change. This rhythmic push contributes to the excitement of jazz rhythm.

THE RED GARLAND PATTERN

Red Garland was a pianist famous for his work in the legendary Miles Davis' Quintet from 1955-58. He frequently plays this comping rhythm on the group's recordings, like *'Round Midnight* and *Relaxin'*.

The *Red Garland* comping pattern places chords on the "and of two" and the "and of four." Notice that these chords directly precede the measure's strongest beats, one and three.

Like the *Charleston*, the offbeat chords must anticipate the next chord symbol. In jazz, always play the chord that's about to arrive rather than the chord that's just passed.

To play this rhythm correctly, start by playing an eighth note *before* the slashes, which could be before the piece even technically begins! A measure that looks like:

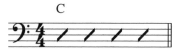

…is correctly played as:

…even though the first eighth note is outside the boundaries of the measure.

RHYTHMIC NOTATION

Pieces sometimes require a specific rhythm. In this case, the desired rhythm is notated with *x*'s on the staff's middle line. These rhythms are commonly called "hits" because the piano, bass and drums often "hit" the chord at the same time. The following indicates a C chord on beat three of a measure:

Play the chord on the beat indicated:

Rhythmic notation can also be used to express more complex rhythms:

When multiple x's are indicated for a single chord symbol, repeat the most recent chord symbol as many times as indicated:

The x notes can do everything that regular notes can – they can have articulation, slurs, dots, and eighth-note beams. Hits can have any of the rhythmic values of normal notes:

The *Charleston* and *Red Garland* comping patterns as well as "hit" notation serve as the foundation for rhythm in this book. The "Rhythm Revisited" section (see p. 62) discusses how to vary these rhythms and how to comp appropriately in other styles and meters.

CHAPTER 2
MAJOR TRIADS

A **triad** is a three-note chord. It helps to recall that most "tri" words involve groups of three: *triangle, triceratops, tricycle, tripod.* Triads are an important building block of traditional Western harmony. Solidifying our knowledge of triads will help us learn more complex chords.

Each note is named based on its position in the scale, except the first note of the scale, which gets a special name, the "root." To form a **major triad**, combine the root, third, and fifth note of a major scale:

We're combining odd numbered notes (1, 3, 5) because these notes create harmony together, whereas combining even and odd numbered notes creates tension. Chords are typically formed by selecting every second note from a scale.

Find an A♭ major triad on the piano.

The most prevalent symbol for a major triad is the letter name of the root note – for a C triad, simply write "C" Here are all of the possible ways to indicate a C major triad*:

C   C^tri   C^triad   C^△

*Because jazz music evolved organically, without any definitive person or organization creating its rules, different musicians sometimes use different symbols to represent the same thing. This book shares all of the possible symbols for a chord, but uses the most common symbols in the pieces and exercises.

MAJOR TRIAD GROUPS

Noticing how each triad lies on the keyboard will help you find triads quickly:

➤ **All White Keys:** Three major triads are all on the white keys: C, F, and G.

➤ **White/Black/White:** Three major triads have the outside fingers on white keys and the middle finger on a black key: D, E, and A.

➤ **Black/White/Black:** Three major triads are the opposite – they have outside fingers on the black keys and the middle finger on a white key: D♭, E♭, and A♭.

➤ **Unique:** And three of them are simply unique: G♭ Major has all black keys. B♭ Major and B Major just have to be memorized.

TO THE SHED!

1) **Complete the Chord:** Supply the missing third for these major triads:

2) **Mismatch:** Label each triad with the appropriate symbol. Then, recalling the four groups of triads, circle the triad that doesn't belong and write the correct triad in the provided measure.

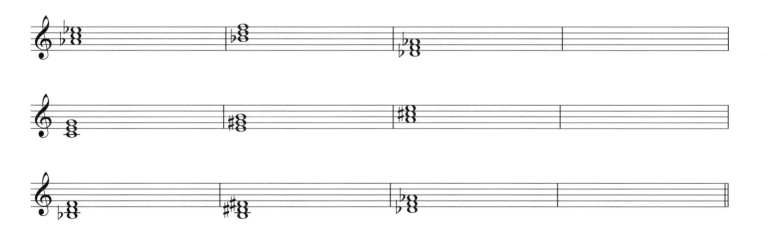

3) **Sudoku:** Fill in the following puzzle so that each vertical row and horizontal column forms a triad (the order of the notes doesn't matter.)

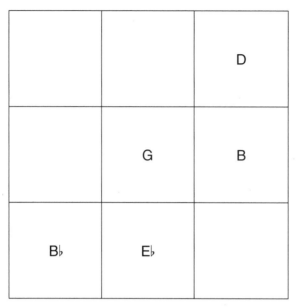

		D
	G	B
B♭	E♭	

4) **Chords/Melodies:** Name the triad outlined by the melody in each measure. In some cases, you'll have to move some notes up or down an octave to find the correct triad.

Just Tri Me

Unrealized Version

Just Tri Me
Realized Version

For all pieces in the book, try to keep the lowest note of your left-hand chord between middle C and the C below middle C. If you get too high, you won't hear the harmony. If you get too low, it will sound too muddy.

CHAPTER 3
MAJOR SEVENTH CHORDS

In the previous chapter, we combined the root, third, and fifth of a major scale to create a major triad.

The **Major Seventh Chord** adds the seventh note of the major scale to the major triad to create a four-note chord. Notice that we're continuing our trend of selecting every second note from the scale:

Chords are named after the scale from which they're built. The major seventh chord built from an E♭ Major scale is called an "E♭ Major seventh" chord. Three different symbols can indicate major seventh chords:

$$E♭maj7 \qquad E♭△7 \qquad E♭M7$$

Find major seventh chords in A and B Major.

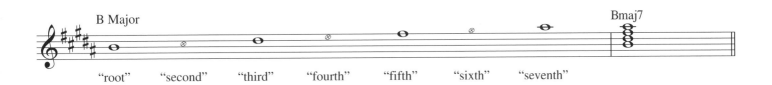

Take a moment to play and listen carefully to the sound of the B Major seventh chord.

It's very pretty, right? Now play just the two outside notes (B and A#). They are very dissonant, that is, ugly or tense sounding. They sound this way because, even though you're playing them far apart the two notes are right next to each other on the keyboard.

The dissonance of these two notes is softened by the notes in between. You can listen for this dissonance to confirm that you're playing the correct notes for a major seventh chord.

TO THE SHED!

1) **Grouping:** Create groups of major seventh chords like we did for major triads in Chapter 2. The first category is filled out for you:

All White Two are on all white keys:

Alternating Black/White Three alternate (from bottom) black-white-black-white:

Alternating White/Black Three alternate (from bottom) white-black-white-black:

One Black Key Two have only one black key:

Three Black Keys Two have three black keys:

2) **Complete the Chord:** Fill in the middle two notes to change these dissonant intervals into nice-sounding major seventh chords. Next, write the chord symbol above the chord:

3) **Mismatch:** Which one doesn't belong? Label the major seventh chords and determine which chord in each group isn't a major seventh chord:

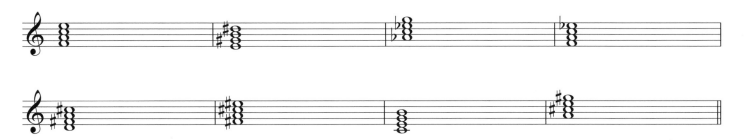

Slinky

Unrealized Version

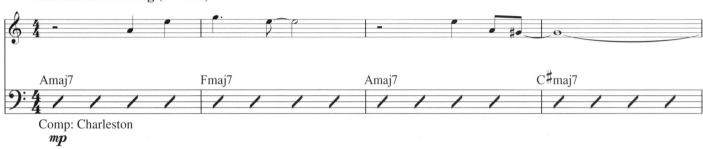

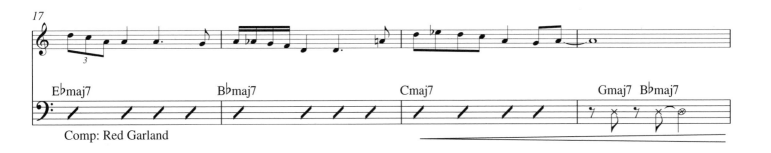

Comp: Red Garland

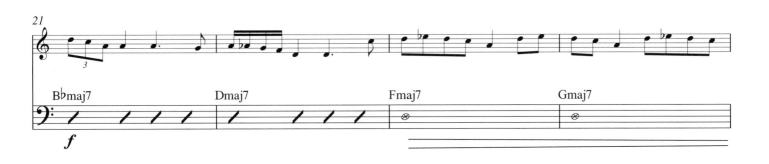

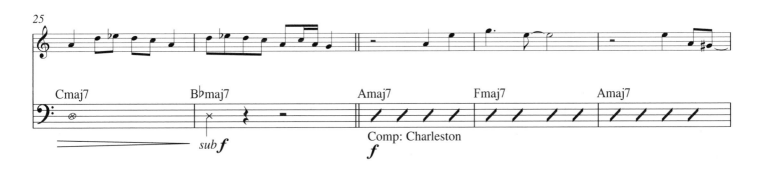

sub *f*

Comp: Charleston
f

Medium-slow Swing (♩ = 100)

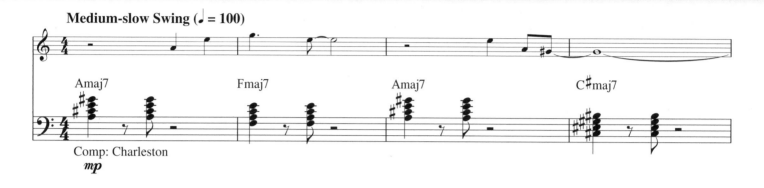

Comp: Charleston

mp

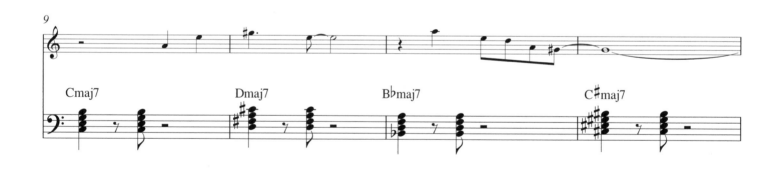

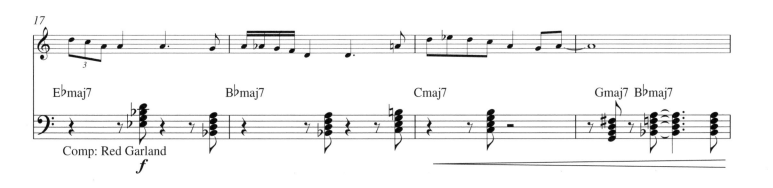

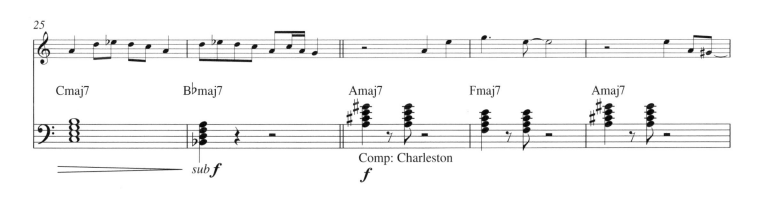

Spinning
Unrealized Version

Medium - straight eighths (♩ = 160)

ritard to end

CHAPTER 4
DOMINANT SEVENTH CHORDS

The **Dominant Seventh Chord** is important in all kinds of music. It's found equally in classical, jazz, blues, and popular music. It's a very tense chord that demands resolution to a more stable sound.

Dominant seventh chords differ from major seventh chords by only one note. To find a dominant seventh chord, find a major seventh chord and lower the seventh (the top note) by one half-step. Notice that this new seventh is now *two* half-steps below the chord's root.

Both the major and dominant seventh chords are built by adding a fourth note to a major triad. You might say they're from the same musical family.

Outside notes of E♭ Major Seventh

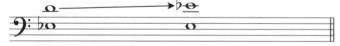

Outside notes of E♭ Dominant Seventh

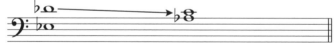

The universal symbol for a dominant seventh chord is simply the root note followed by a "7", like D7 or C#7. Find A♭ and B♭ dominant seventh chords:

The dominant seventh chord's tension is created by the relationship between its third and seventh. These two notes form an interval called a "tritone", which perfectly divides the octave. The tritone – named because it spans three whole-steps, often referred to as "tones" – is one of the tensest intervals in music. Play the tritone by itself:

You can probably hear why ancient cultures thought of the tritone as "the devil's interval." Listen for the tension of the tritone to confirm you're forming dominant seventh chord correctly.

TO THE SHED!

1) **Fill-in:** Supply the missing chord or chord symbol in the music below:

2) **Mixer:** Write the correct chord for each chord symbol. Notice that some are major triads, some are major seventh chords, and some are dominant seventh chords:

D♭maj7	E♭7	F	A7	E♭maj7	Bmaj7	B♭7	D7	A	A♭maj7

3) **Riddles:** A) What two chords (one major seventh and one dominant seventh) both have the note B♭ as the seventh?

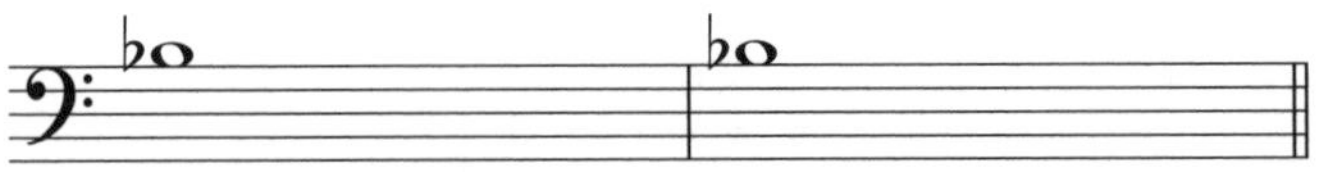

B) What four dominant seventh chords all have the note E as part of the chord?

4) **Grouping:** Complete the chart below?

Dominant 7th chords on all white keys (one)	G7
Dominant 7th chords with only one black key (five)	
Dominant 7th chords with two black keys (three)	
Dominant 7th chords with three black keys (three)	

World Domination
Unrealized Version

"N.C." below stands for "No Chord" – in other words, don't play anything!

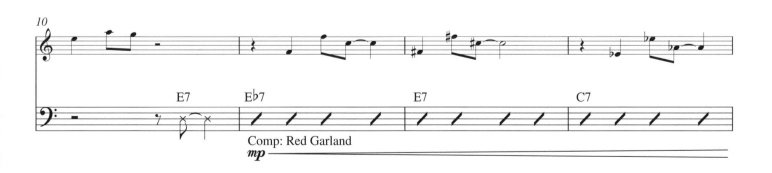

Medium Shuffle (♩ = 140)

Comp: Charleston
mf

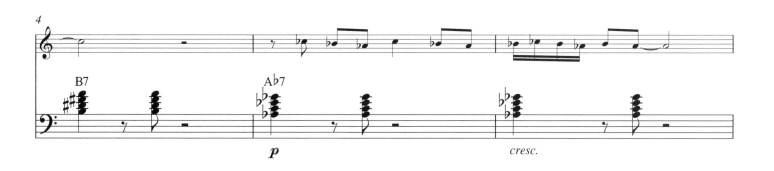

p   *cresc.*

f

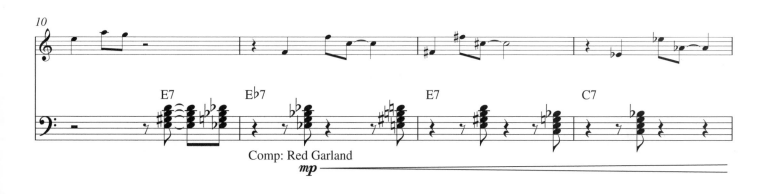

Comp: Red Garland
mp

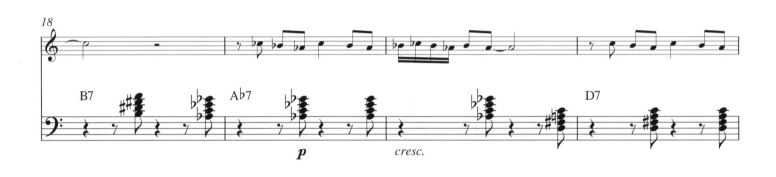

Sunrise
Unrealized Version

Sunrise
Realized Version

CHAPTER 5
MINOR TRIADS

Both major seventh and dominant seventh chords are created by adding a fourth note to a major triad. Before learning a third type of seventh chord, we need to briefly study minor triads.

To form a minor triad, combine the root, third, and fifth of any minor scale.*

How does this triad differ from the major triad in the same key?

The third (middle note) of the minor triad is a half-step lower than the third of the major triad, but the two are otherwise identical. The lowered third is called a **minor third** whereas the "regular" third is called a **major third**.

Another way to form a minor triad, then, is to form a major triad and lower its third:

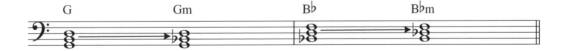

Minor triads are typically indicated by a lower case "m" after the root note. Below are other possible symbols for a minor triad:

Fm   F-   Fmin

It's generally accepted that major chords sound "happy" whereas minor chords sound "sad". Take a moment to listen to the chords' different characters and decide for yourself.

*Since only the sixth and seventh scale degrees differ between natural minor, harmonic minor, and melodic minor, it doesn't matter which minor scale you use.

Practice grouping the minor triads by white-key/black-key hand position:

Three minor triads use all white keys	Dm, Em, Am
Three minor triads use black keys on the outside	D♭m, G♭m, A♭m
Three minor triads use black keys on the inside	Cm, Fm, Gm
Three minor triads are unique	B♭m, Bm, E♭m

TO THE SHED!

1) **Word search:** Find all six minor triads in the word search below. The notes can be horizontal, vertical, or diagonal in any order.

A♭	F	A	D
D	C♭	G♭	C
G♭	C	E♭	A♭
A	G	B♭	D

2) **Major Chord, Minor Chord:** Each measure contains one minor chord and one major chord. Label both with the correct chord symbol and circle the minor chord in each group.

3) **Mixer:** Write the correct triad for each chord symbol given. Be careful – there are both major and minor triads included.

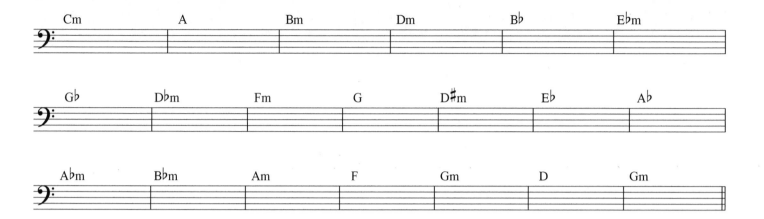

4) **Riddle:** Use the clues below to answer the following riddle.

Why did the piano key make a buzzing sound?

Because it was

_____   _____   _____   _____.

| 3rd of an F# minor chord | 5th of an E minor chord | 3rd of a C# minor chord | 3rd of a C major chord |

CHAPTER 6

MINOR SEVENTH CHORDS

To transform a minor triad into a **Minor Seventh Chord**, add the note two half-steps below the chord's root. This lowered seventh, the **minor seventh**, is the same note used to complete dominant seventh chords (see Chapter 4).

Find minor seventh chords in A and F.

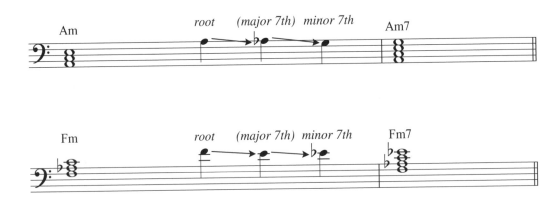

Minor seventh chords are most commonly indicated with a lower case "m" and a "7". Here are all of the possible symbols for a minor seventh chord:

Fm7   F-7   Fmi7   Fmin7

Compare the minor seventh chord to the seventh chords we've already learned:

Only the thirds and sevenths differentiate these three chords – the roots and the fifths are identical. Remember this fact – it will become important in later chapters when we begin to form voicings.

Two notes differentiate the major seventh and minor seventh chords. The major seventh chord becomes a minor seventh chord when you lower (flat) the third and the seventh of the chord.

Only one note differentiates the dominant and minor seventh chords. A dominant seventh chord becomes a minor seventh chord when you lower (flat) the third.

This chart reviews how to create each type of seventh chord:

Chord Type	3rd	7th
Major Seventh	Major	Major
Dominant Seventh	Major	Minor (lowered)
Minor Seventh	Minor (lowered)	Minor (lowered)

TO THE SHED!

1) **Complete the Chord:** Write the correct seventh for the following chords. Notice that the first line consists of all minor seventh chords and the second line mixes major, dominant, and minor seventh chords.

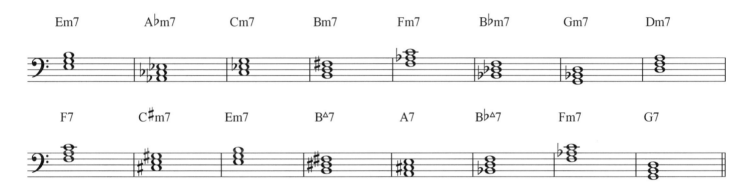

2) **Scramble:** Unscramble the following groups of notes to create minor seventh chords. Write the correct chord symbol over the measure (you will have to change the octaves of some of the notes).

3) **Fill-in:** Supply the missing chords or chord symbols for each measure.

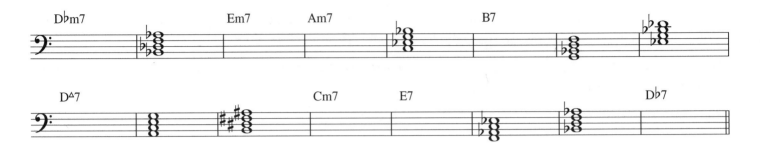

4) **Riddle:** Answer each clue to solve the riddle: "What do you get when you drop a piano down a mine shaft?"

A) Start with the minor seventh chord that has E♭ as its seventh _____m7

B) Move to the minor seventh chord that has the answer to (A) as its third _____m7

C) Find the major seventh chord that has the answer to (B) as its seventh _____Δ7

D) Find the dominant seventh chord that has the answer to (C) as its third _____7

E) The answer is the minor triad that has the answer to (D) as its third _____

Slow Walk

Unrealized Version

Comp: Red Garland

Comp: Red Garland

Twilight Strut
Unrealized Version

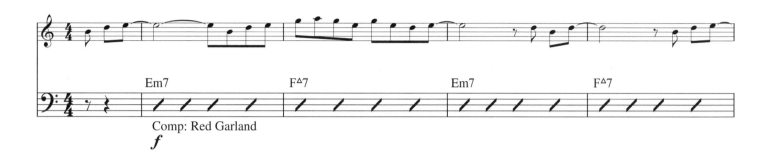

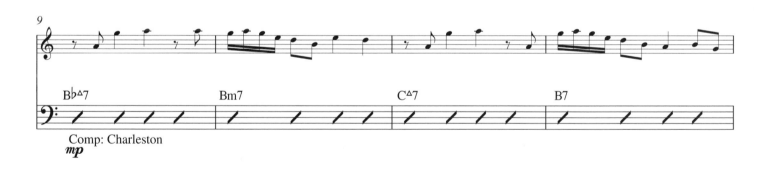

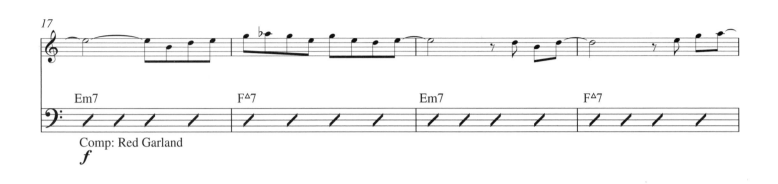

Comp: Red Garland

f

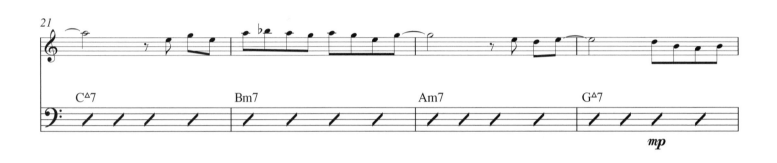

mp

Comp: Charleston

p

Twilight Strut
Realized Version

Comp: Red Garland

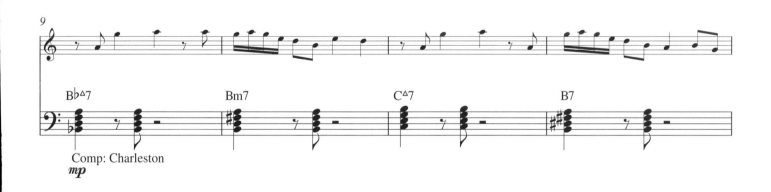

Comp: Charleston

Comp: Red Garland

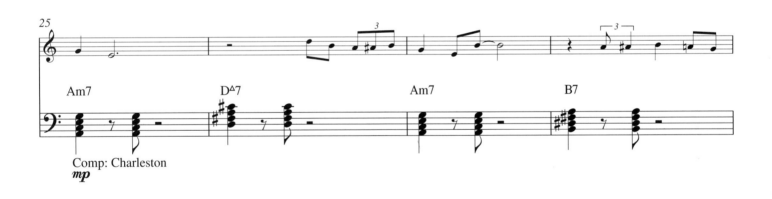

Comp: Charleston
mp

CHAPTER 7
THE ii-V-I PROGRESSION

The **ii-V-I Progression** (pronounced: "two-five-one") is the principle building block of traditional jazz harmony. Any pianist who can thoroughly master this short progression and its variants will make significant progress towards being able to instantaneously play the chords in a piece of jazz music.

HOW IT WORKS

The ii-V-I progression is named for three important scale degrees of the major scale:

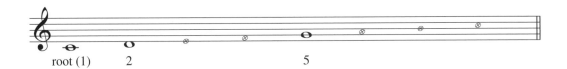

To create a ii-V-I, build four-note chords from each of these notes. For the ii ("two") chord, select alternating notes starting from the second note of the scale.

Next, for the V ("five") chord, select every second note starting from the fifth note of the scale. You'll have to repeat some of the scale's notes to complete the chord:

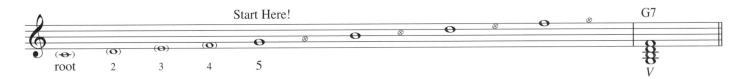

Lastly, for the I ("one") chord, select every other note starting from the root:

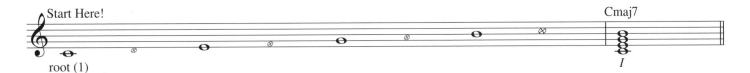

If you do this correctly, you'll form a minor seventh, dominant seventh, and major seventh chord, respectively. When you play these three chords in order, you're playing a ii-V-I progression:

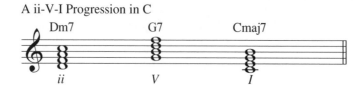

Now that you understand how it works, take a shortcut: no matter what the key, the chords of a ii-V-I progression will be a minor seventh, a dominant seventh, and a major seventh chord formed from the second, fifth, and root of a major scale, respectively.

Important: ii-V-I progressions are named for the key of the root (the "I" chord), not the key of the first chord (the "ii" chord). For instance the above example above is in C even though it begins on Dm7.

Find a ii-V-I in A♭ Major.

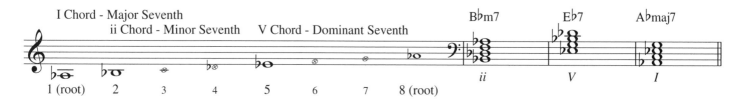

TO THE SHED!

1) **Fill-in:** Supply the missing information for these ii-V-I progressions

Key of _____: Em7 - _____ - D△7	Key of _____: Cm7 - F7 - B♭△7
Key of _____: A♭m7 - D♭7 - G♭△7	Key of A: Bm7 - E7 - _____
Key of B: C♯m7 - _____ - B△7	Key of C♯: _____ - G♯7 - _____

2) **Missing Pieces:** Supply the missing chords in the following progressions:

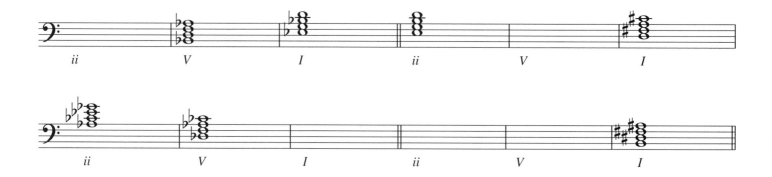

3) **Search Committee:** Find and circle the six ii-V-I progressions hidden vertically, horizontally, and diagonally (forwards or backwards) in the puzzle below:

Fm7	G7	A♭m7	D♭7	G♭7	E♭m7
B7	B♭7	D♭7	G♭△7	F△7	A♭7
E△7	A△7	E♭△7	D♭7	C7	D♭△7
C△7	E7	A△7	A♭m7	Gm7	A7
F♯7	Bm7	E7	A△7	D♭7	Dm7
G△7	Gm7	C7	F△7	C7	G♭△7

VOICE LEADING

Voice leading describes the smoothness of the movement from one chord to the next. The term comes from vocal music in which a different person sings each note of a chord. Each vocalist's melody must *lead* smoothly from one chord to the next so that the parts aren't too difficult to sing.

When two chords move with *good voice leading*, every note is either the same or only a step (whole or half) away from its corresponding note in the previous chord.

To create good voice leading, chords are often put in inversions. An **inversion** is a reordering of a chord's notes so that a note *other than the root* is placed at the bottom.

Bad Voice Leading:

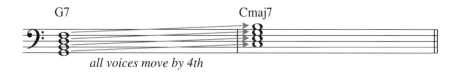

all voices move by 4th

Good Voice Leading:

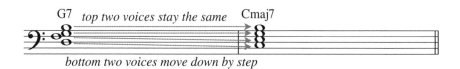

bottom two voices move down by step

In the example above, the G7 is placed in inversion, with D as the lowest note. With this change, each of the chord's notes is either the same as or adjacent to its related note in C Major.

VOICE LEADING FOR ii-V-I'S

Since ii-V-I progressions are so prevalent, learning and digesting patterns for good voice leading for the progression is crucial. Practice playing the "ii" and "I" (the first and last) chords in root position and placing the "V" chord in inversion with the fifth on bottom, like this:

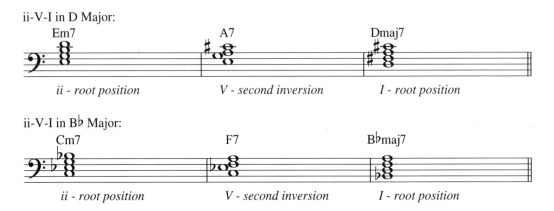

PRACTICING ii-V-I'S

A major step towards playing jazz piano fluidly is being able to recall ii-V-I progressions *instantaneously* in every key.

Below are some exercises for practicing the progression. *Always* practice with a metronome, even if you're practicing at an excruciatingly slow tempo. Also, be sure to notice how your fingers move – muscle memory and quick physical recall helps make playing the chords fast and automatic.

➤ **Metamorphosis**

After each ii-V-I, transform the "I" chords into a minor seventh chord to become the new "ii" (it takes two sets to get through all keys):

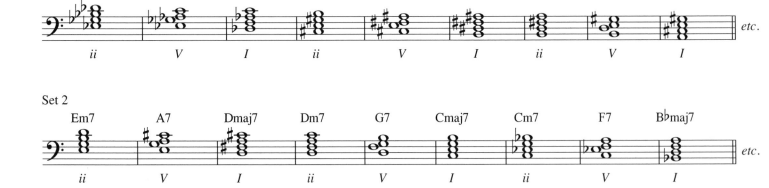

➤ **Circle of Fifths**

After finishing a ii-V-I, play the next ii-V-I in the key a fifth above the previous key. Remember: move a fifth between each of the "I" chords, not between the "I" chord and the next "ii" chord:

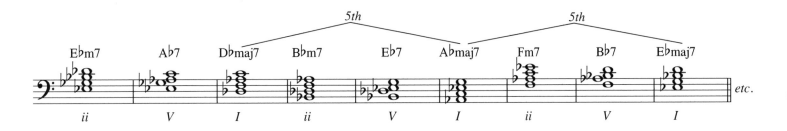

➤ **Chromatic Climb**

After finishing a ii-V-I, play the next ii-V-I in the key one-half step above the previous key:

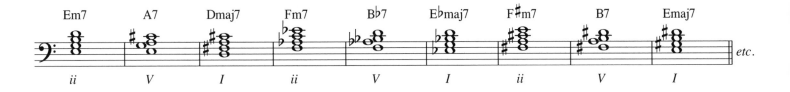

If you need help figuring out the rest of these patterns, the full progressions are provided in the book's appendix (pp. 149-150).

The Easy Life
Unrealized Version

Comp: Red Garland

Comp: Charleston
mf

The Easy Life
Realized Version

Medium fast Swing (♩ = 160)

Comp: Charleston

Don't Bother Me
Unrealized Version

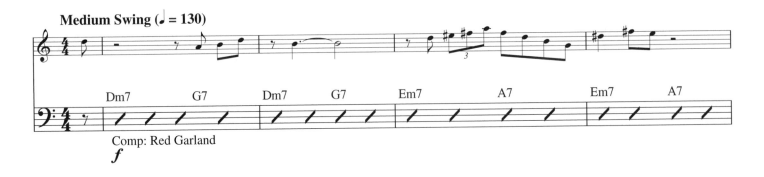

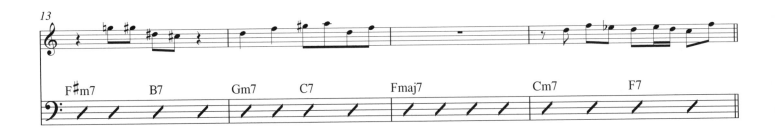

Round Dance
Unrealized Version

CHAPTER 8
RHYTHM REVISITED

Chapter 1 introduced the **Charleston** and **Red Garland** comping patterns. This chapter discusses two ways to vary these rhythms. It also presents two new patterns: traditional rhythms for Brazilian dances and jazz waltz styles.

VARIATION 1: VARY THE LENGTH

A simple way to achieve rhythmic variety is to vary the length of chords. For example, the *Charleston* sounds very different if the note on the downbeat is held until the note on the offbeat is played.

Think of this variant as a trap that's loaded and ready to spring. When playing the first chord, move your forearm slowly downwards and then spring up for the accented chord on the off-beat.

Similarly, try holding *all* of the chords in the *Red Garland* pattern. This is a great way to create excitement because it highlights the tension of the succession of off-beats. Make sure to give each chord a strong accent:

Experiment on your own with other combinations of long and short notes to vary these simple patterns.

VARIATION 2: ADD A DOWNBEAT NOTE

Another way to vary these patterns is to add a chord on the downbeat directly preceding an off-beat chord. Since the downbeat leads into the off-beat, it won't interrupt the forward momentum of the music.

When playing the *Charleston* pattern, pair a note on beat two with the accented stab on the "and of two". Make sure there's no space in between the two eighth-notes – that is, don't allow the key to spring all the way back up before re-striking.

The chord on beat two comes too early to anticipate the chord symbol written on beat three. Therefore, this variation, requires different chords for the two consecutive eighth notes.

Similarly, when playing the *Red Garland* pattern, experiment with adding downbeat chords on either beat two or beat four to add rhythmic variety. Aim for a mix of beats to provide the most rhythmic diversity:

Make sure to accent the off-beats on these patterns. If you accent the downbeats, you'll lose the rhythmic lift that gives jazz its exciting momentum.

BOSSA NOVA/SAMBA PATTERN

Bossa Nova and **Samba** are two dances from Brazil that are frequently incorporated in jazz pieces. *Samba* is a fast dance whereas *bossa nova* is a medium or slow dance. You can use similar rhythmic patterns for both – only the tempo will be different. Unlike swing rhythm, which uses uneven eighth notes, these styles have **straight eighths** (rhythmically even notes).

These dances have rich and long traditions with countless variations and intricacies. Here's a good pattern to use until you learn more about these dances:

Unlike the swing patterns we've learned, the *bossa nova/samba* pattern is two measures long. Like the swing patterns, the chords are anticipated, that is, they change an eighth note before the written indication.

Here are some more examples:

WALTZ PATTERNS

The *Waltz* is a dance that takes place in $\frac{3}{4}$ time. When playing a *Waltz*, place chords on the downbeat and on the "and of two" (the middle of the measure). Since most chord changes occur on these beats, you shouldn't have to worry about anticipations:

CHAPTER 9
THE NINTH

So far, we've discussed jazz harmony in terms of four-note chords – chords with a root, third, fifth, and seventh. However, a fifth note – **the ninth** – plays an important role in jazz harmony.

Play a C Major Scale and continue beyond the eighth note, the repetition of the root. The ninth note repeats the second scale degree.

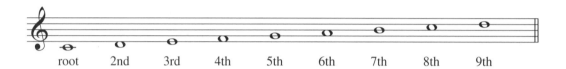

Remember that chords are created by selecting every second note of the scale. The ninth is the next logical note to add to a chord after the seventh.

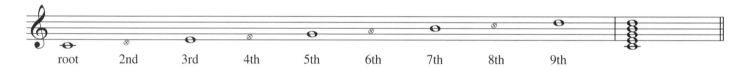

Because all common scales have the same second scale degree, the ninth will always be the same tone – a whole-step above the root – regardless of whether it's used for a major, minor, or dominant seventh chord.

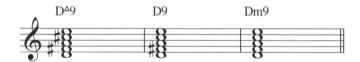

Important: Because the above chords utilize the ninth, the chord symbols above contain a "9" instead of a "7". However, even if the chord symbol only indicates a seventh ("Dm7", for example), you are permitted – and typically expected – to play the ninth. When a symbol indicates Dm9 instead of Dm7, the score is being extra specific that you can use the ninth, usually because it is in the melody.

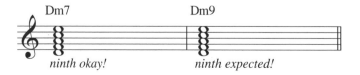

TO THE SHED!

1) What Doesn't Belong: Circle the chord in each group that does not have the correct ninth.

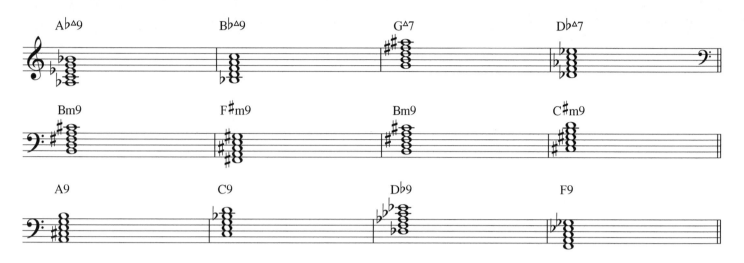

2) Fill-in: Write the ninth for the following chords indicated.

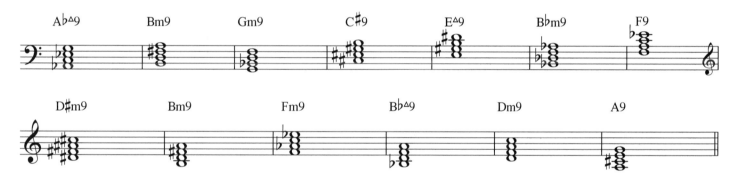

3) Check My Work: Is this chord acceptable for the chord symbol? _____ Why or why not? _____

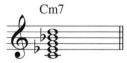

4) Riddle: Use the clues to answer the following riddle.

Why was the farmer a good drummer?

Because he could always keep the

_____   _____   _____   _____ .

| 9th of an Am9 | 9th of a D9 | 7th of of an F#m9 | 20th letter of the alphabet |

CHAPTER 10
SHELL VOICINGS

Although it's convenient to learn about the theory behind different chords by building them "in order," in practice, the notes of a chord can be arranged in many different ways. These rearrangements are called "voicings."

This chapter teaches introduces **Shell Voicings**, voicings that are widely used in jazz.

There are two types of shell voicings called "Type A" and "Type B." The **Type A** voicing places the third on the bottom, and then (in ascending order) includes the seventh, ninth, and fifth.*

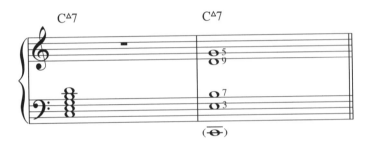

The seventh is at the bottom of the **Type B** voicing. The other chord tones used (in ascending order) are the third, fifth, ninth.

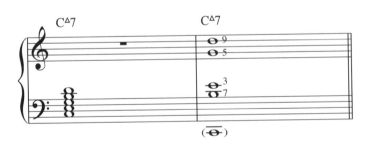

To hear how these voicings sound, hit a low C, hold the pedal down, and play the voicing while the C is still ringing. You should hear a rich, evenly-spaced sound, very different from the cluttered chords from the previous chapters.

Please notice a few things about these voicings:

- They *don't* include the root! Thus far, we've used the root as an anchor to remind us what chord we're playing. However, in a jazz band, the bass plays the root, so it's superfluous for the pianist to play it as well.

- They require both hands! Usually, in a jazz band, someone else is playing the melody, so you can use both of your hands to play the chords. We'll explore chord voicings that you can use when you need to play a melody with your right hand in Chapter 13 (p. 110)

- The third and seventh are always in the left hand, on the bottom of the voicing. Remember that the third and seventh define whether the chords are major, minor, or dominant. Because they're so critical to defining the chords, these two tones are always placed nearest to the bass and are called **"essential tones"**.

- The right hand always plays the fifth and ninth. We can call these **"color tones"** because they don't define the chord's type, but make it sound richer or fuller or more harmonious.

* The root is included in the examples in parentheses. This is only for reference – *do not play the root* when comping – it's not part of the voicing.

Find Type A & Type B voicings for the following chords. It's helpful to find the root position voicing first and then rearrange the notes to form a shell voicing. *Don't worry* – this will be tedious in the beginning, but it will quickly become automatic with some practice!

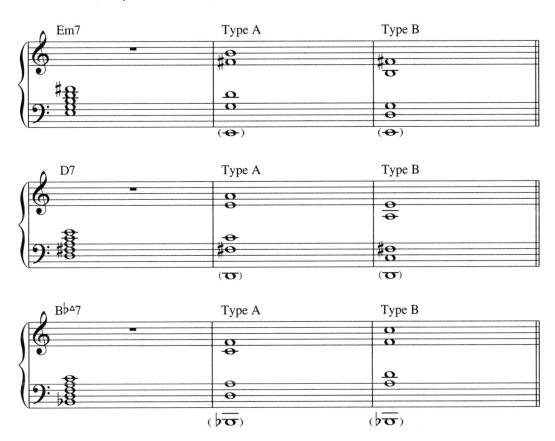

In order to make sure that the voicing isn't too high or too low, keep its lowest note between "middle C" and the C below "middle C."

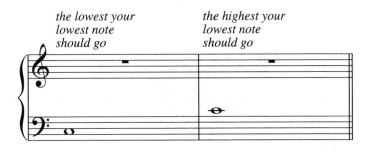

[Musical staff with: Eb△7, Too high!, Too low!, Just right!]

VOICING TRIADS IN SHELL VOICINGS

Even though most chords you'll encounter in jazz pieces are seventh chords, occasionally, you'll need to form voicings for triads.* For a **Type A** voicing, replace the seventh with the fifth and the ninth with the root. For a **Type B** voicing, replace both the seventh and the ninth with the root.

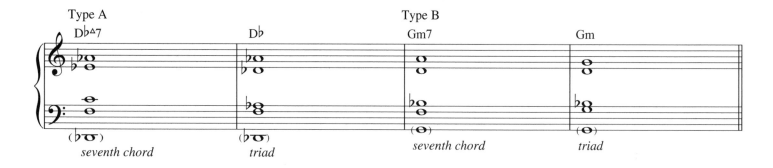

Type A   Db△7   Db   Type B   Gm7   Gm

(bo)   (bo)   (o)   (o)
seventh chord   triad   seventh chord   triad

TO THE SHED!

1) **A or B:** Identify the voicing as either Type A or Type B.

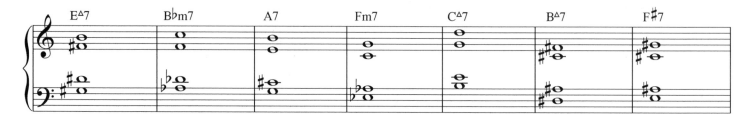

*Remember that you'll be able to recognize triads because they won't have a number (like a ^{7} or ^{9}) after the chord symbol (Gm^7 is a seventh chord; Gm is a triad).

2) **Transformations:** First write the root position voicing in the space provided, then write both the Type A and Type B voicings. Note the chord tones next to each note.

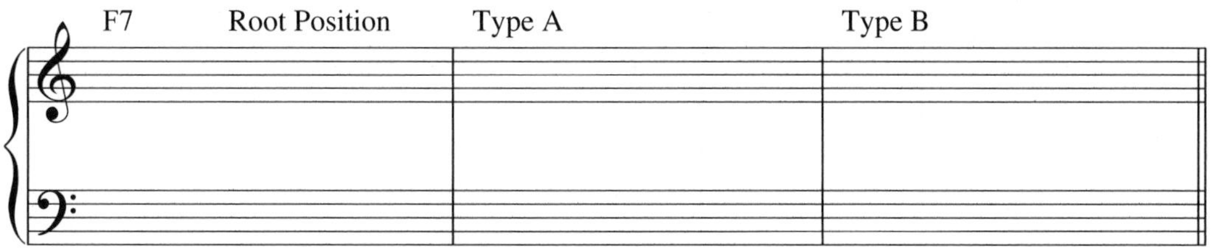

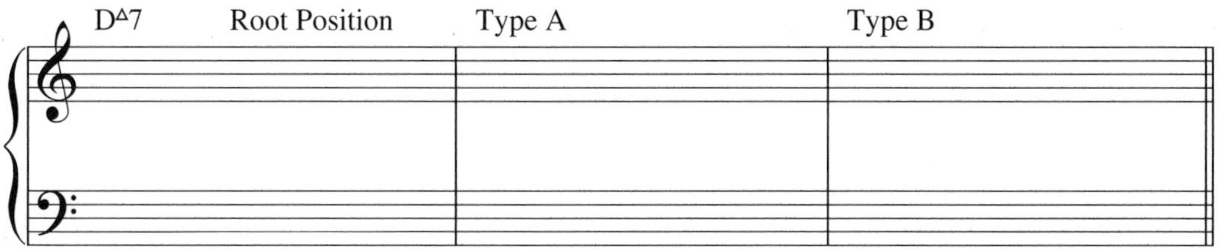

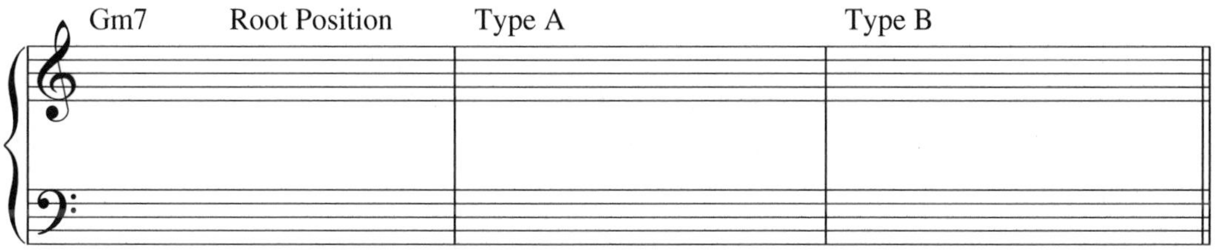

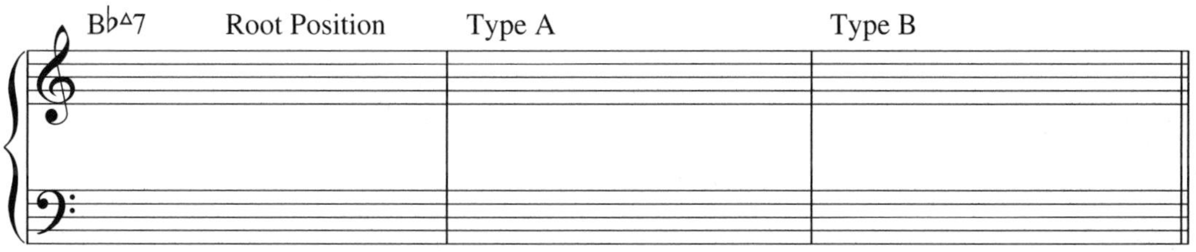

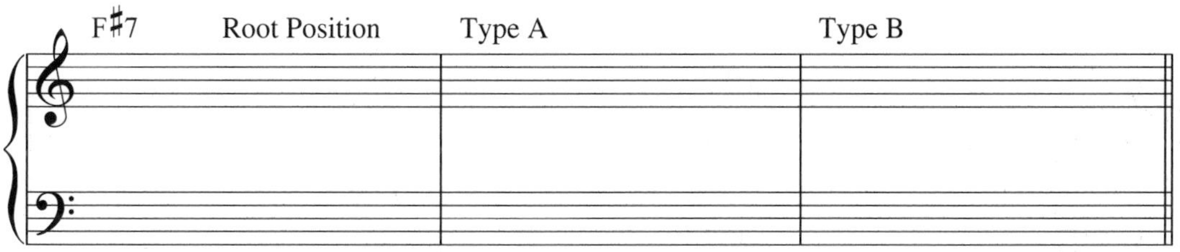

F7   Root Position   Type A   Type B

D△7   Root Position   Type A   Type B

Gm7   Root Position   Type A   Type B

B♭△7   Root Position   Type A   Type B

F♯7   Root Position   Type A   Type B

3) **Fill-in:** Write the indicated voicing for each chord symbol.

Dm7	Type B	E△7	Type B	A♭7	Type A	B7	Type B	E♭m7	Type A	F♯m7	Type A	F7	Type A

A♭△7	Type B	C7	Type A	E♭7	Type B	Gm7	Type B	B♭m7	Type A	A7	Type A	F△7	Type B

SHELL VOICINGS IN ii-V-I'S

One of the reasons that shell voicings are very popular with jazz band pianists is that they make playing ii-V-I's very easy. If you learn the finger patterns for shell voicings in the context of ii-V-I's, you'll be able to immediately play most jazz band pieces.

When encountering a ii-V-I progression, you will always *alternate* between Type A and Type B voicings. Either voicing can start the progression so long as each successive voicing changes type.

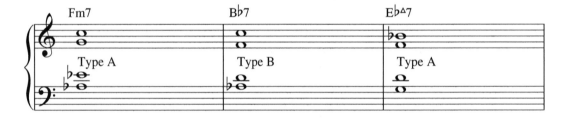

70

You barely have to move your fingers to play these chord progressions successfully. In fact, if you mentally divide the chords into two pairs of notes – the middle two and the outer two notes – you'll notice that only one pair moves at a time:

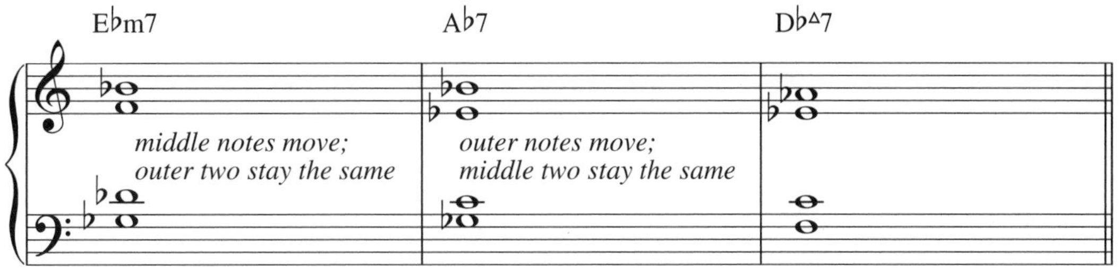

These notes *always* move downward and they always move by step. Find ii-V-I's in a couple of other keys:

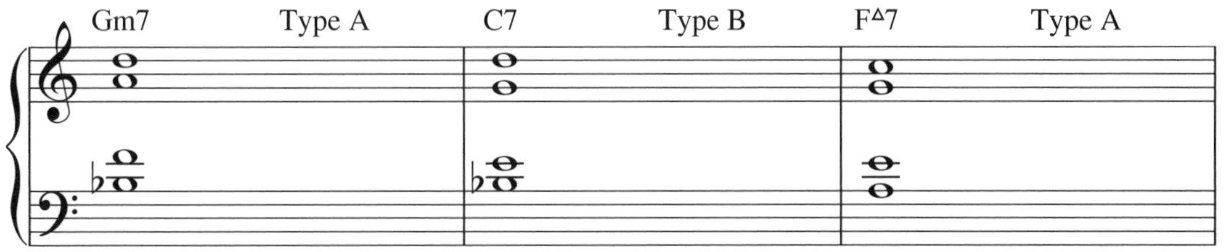

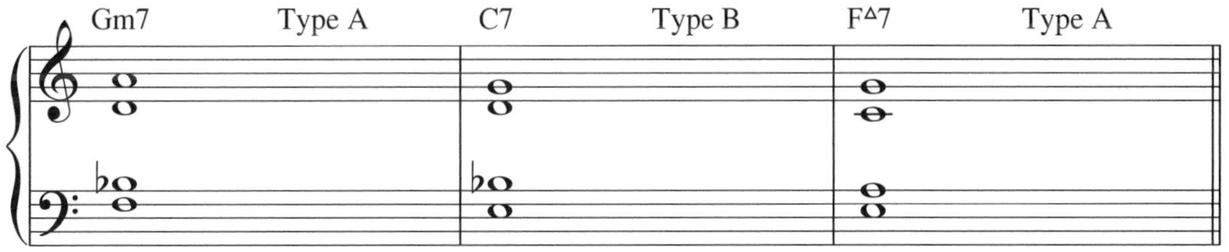

PRACTICING ii–V–I'S

Take the exercise sets we learned in Chapter 7 and apply them to these voicings. Practice each exercise starting both with Type A and Type B voicings to make sure you master all possible combinations.

➤ **Metamorphosis**

After each ii–V–I, transform the "I" chords into a minor seventh chord to become the new "ii" (it takes two sets to get to all keys):

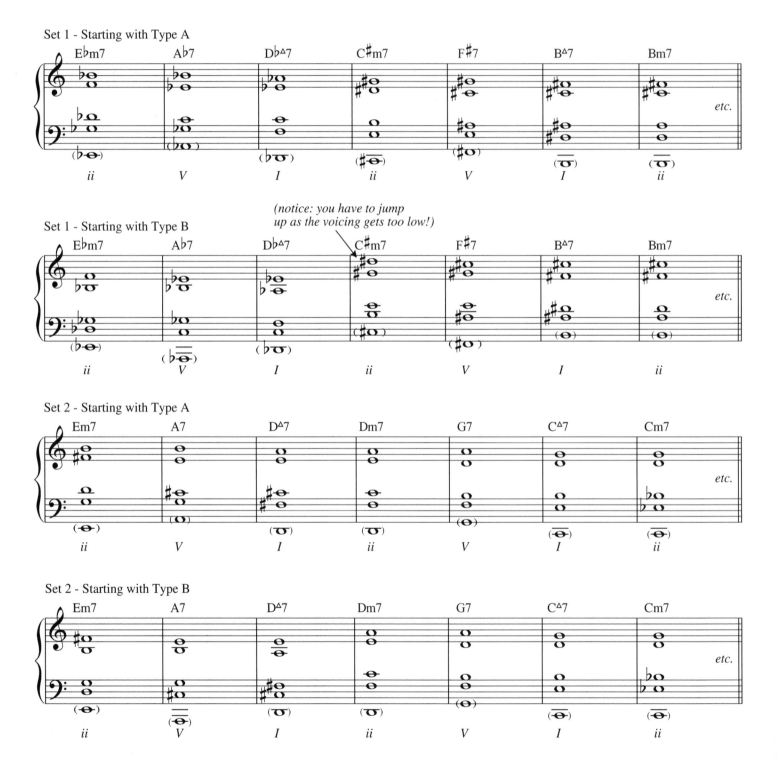

➤ **Circle of Fifths**

After finishing a ii-V-I, play the next ii-V-I in the key a fifth above the previous key. Remember: move a fifth between each of the "I" chords, not between the "I" chord and the next "ii" chord:

Circle of 5ths - Starting with Type A

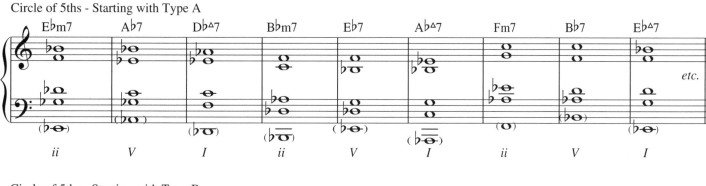

Circle of 5ths - Starting with Type B

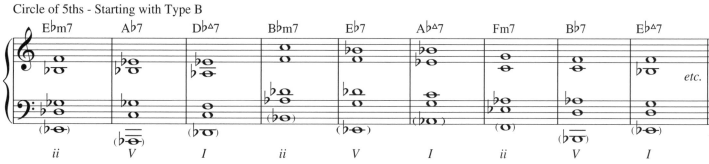

➤ **Chromatic Climb**

After finishing a ii-V-I, play the next ii-V-I in the key a one-half step above the previous key:

Chromatic Climb - Starting with Type A

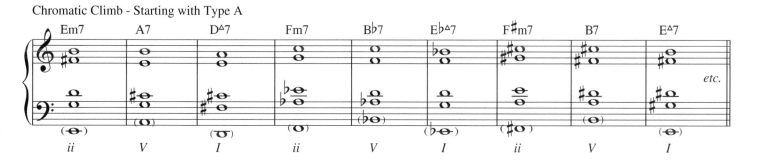

Chromatic Climb - Starting with Type B

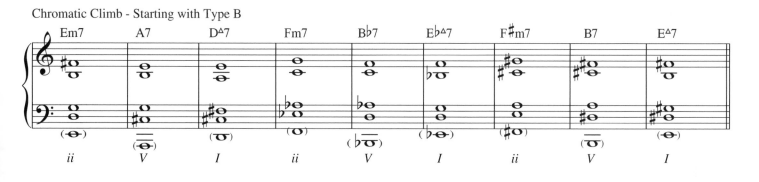

The Easy Life

(Shell Voicing Version)

Unrealized Version

Transform the ii-V-Is you learned for "The Easy Life" in Chapter 7 into shell voicings.

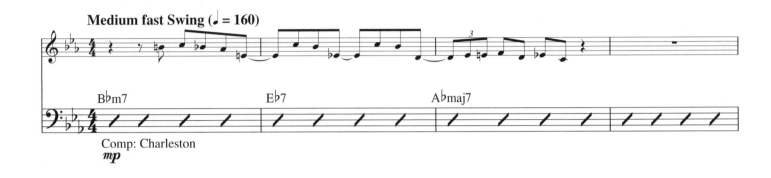

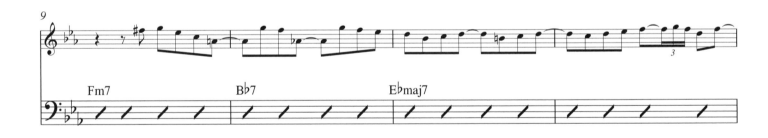

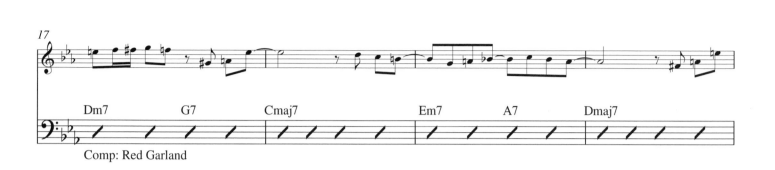

Comp: Red Garland

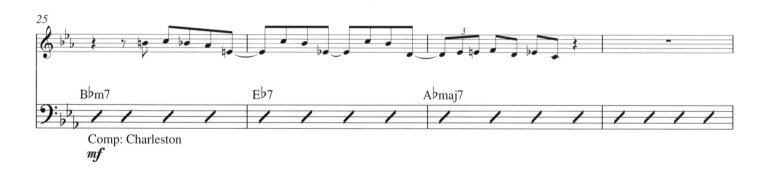

Comp: Charleston

mf

The Easy Life

(Shell Voicing Version)

Realized Version

Feel free to use the information from "Rhythm Revisited" to make creative variations that are different from the realization given here.

Medium fast Swing (♩ = 160)

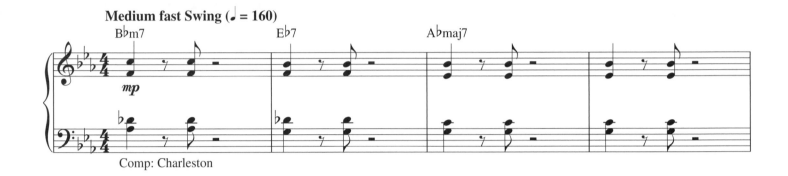

Comp: Charleston

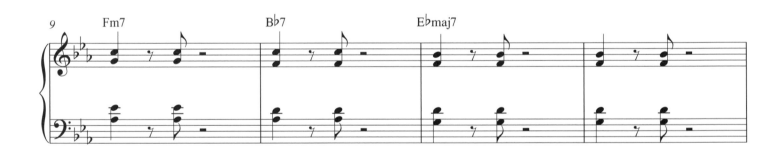

Comp: Red Garland

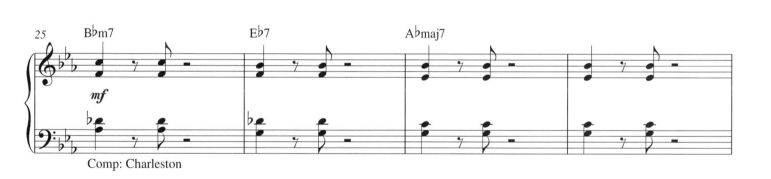

Comp: Charleston

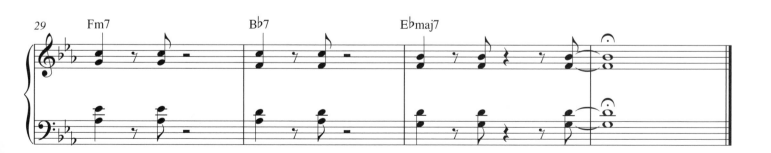

The Punch Line

Unrealized Version

Medium Swing ($\quarternote$ = 126)

G$^\triangle$7   Am7   D7   G$^\triangle$7   Am7   D7

Comp: Red Garland
mf

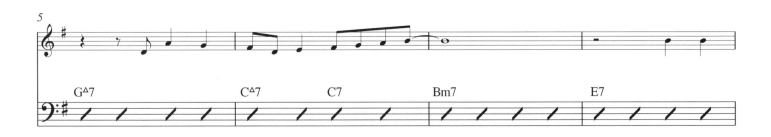

5

G$^\triangle$7   C$^\triangle$7   C7   Bm7   E7

9   **Straight eighths**

Am7   D7   C#m7   F#7   Bm7   E7

Comp: Bossa Nova
p

13

Am7   D7   B♭m7   E♭7   Cm7   F7

78

Comp: Red Garland

Medium Swing (♩ = 126)

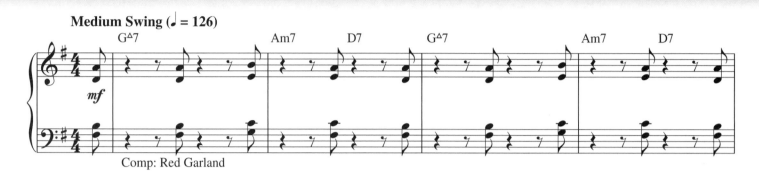

Comp: Red Garland

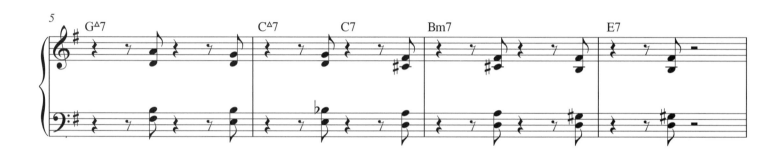

Straight eighths

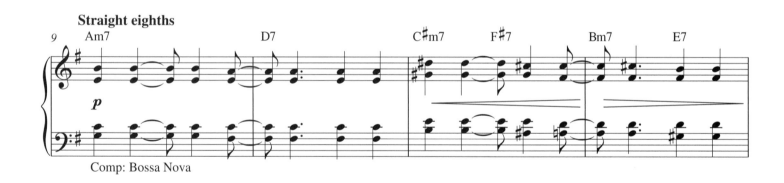

Comp: Bossa Nova

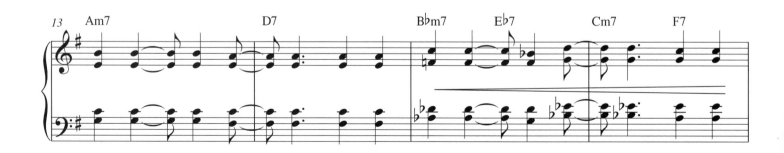

Comp: Red Garland

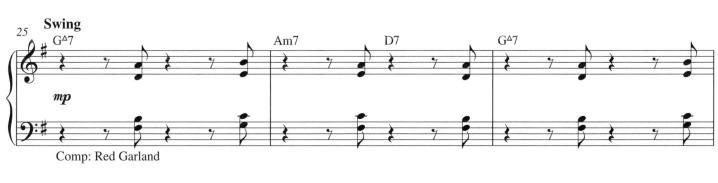

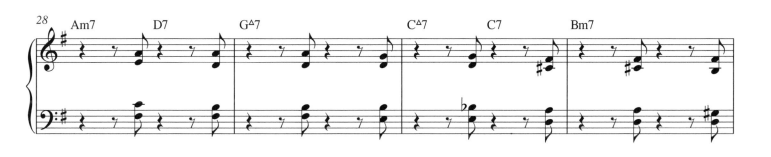

A Lighthouse
Unrealized Version

A Lighthouse
Realized Version

ALTERED TONES

ALTERED TONES

In Chapter 10, we discussed how thirds and the sevenths are **essential tones** because they define if a chord is major, minor, or dominant. We called the fifth and the ninth "**color tones**" because they "shade" or "fill out" the chord's sound.

For dominant chords, the color tones can be lowered or raised by half-steps to create **altered tones**. Play through the chords with altered tones and notice their unique sounds:

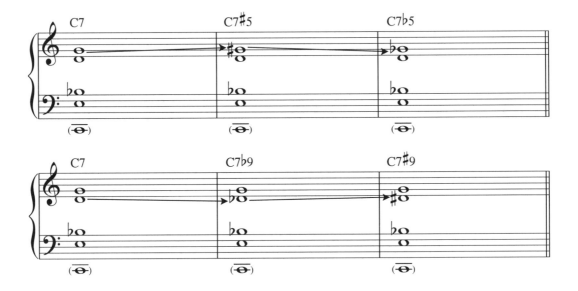

Altered tones can be used in all possible combinations:

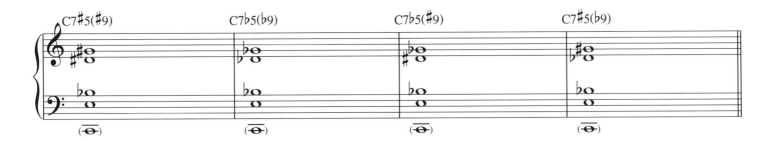

The chord symbols indicate the alterations after the number (usually seven) that describes the chord's sonority. When an alteration is indicated, you *must* alter that note. Typically, an alteration is indicated when an altered tone is used in the melody. Remember that the flats and sharps don't mean that you have to use a flat or sharp note. They're simply directing you to *lower* or *raise* the note as indicated.

Important: You're also free to alter notes when alterations aren't indicated. For example, if you see an E♭7, you can lower the ninth or raise the fifth or perform any combination of alterations. You have this power! Remember two rules, though:

1. You can only freely alter notes of *dominant* chords.

2. The altered tone you choose must not clash with the melody. For example, don't play a flatted ninth if someone in the band is playing a natural ninth.

THE "ALT" CHORD

Sometimes, instead of writing out multiple alterations, a composer will indicate an "alt" chord, such as F7alt. "Alt" means that you must alter (either raise or lower – you get to choose) *both* the fifth and the ninth of the chord.

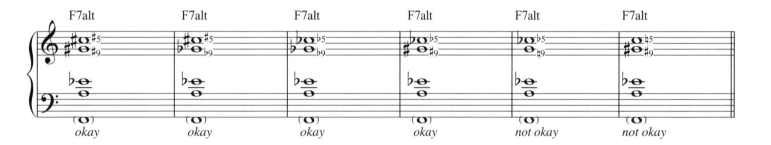

Because altered dominant chords are such a strong part of the jazz sound, it will be highly beneficial to practice all of the ii-V-I patterns using all combinations of altered tones.

TO THE SHED!

1) **Finish the Job:** Add the correct alterations to the chord symbols for the chords given below. Be careful: some might not have any alterations at all.

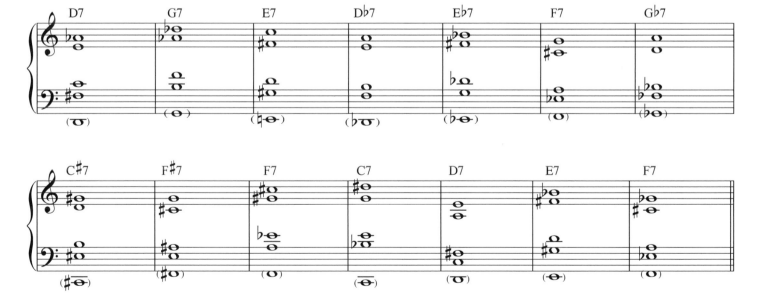

2) **Allowed or Forbidden:** Compare the chord symbols with the melody. Based on the melody notes, will the indicated altered tones be acceptable?

3) **Write it Out:** Write a shell voicing for the following altered chords.

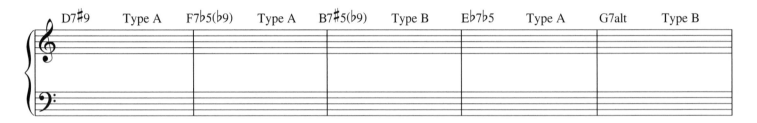

4) **Puzzler:** List all of the dominant chords that use F as an altered tone:

   (1) It's the ♭5 of _____

   (2) It's the ♯5 of _____

   (3) It's the ♭9 of _____

   (4) It's the ♯9 of _____

Unscramble your answers to answer the joke: Where does a flower sleep at night?

_____ _____ _____ _____

The Punch Line
(Altered Tone Version)

Unrealized Version

Last chapter, you learned "The Punchline." Try playing the same tune with the new alterations, noticing how much richer and more colorful the harmony sounds.

Medium Swing (♩ = 126)

Comp: Red Garland
mf

Chords: G△7 | Am7 D7♯5 | G△7 | Am7 D7♭5

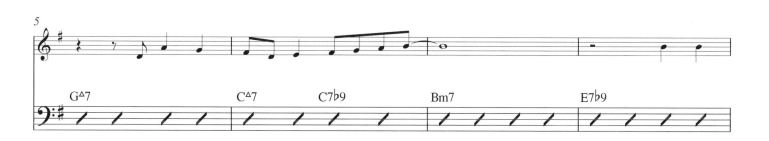

Chords: G△7 | C△7 C7♭9 | Bm7 | E7♭9

Straight eighths

Comp: Bossa Nova
p

Chords: Am7 | D7♭9 | C♯m7 F♯7♯5 | Bm7 E7♭9

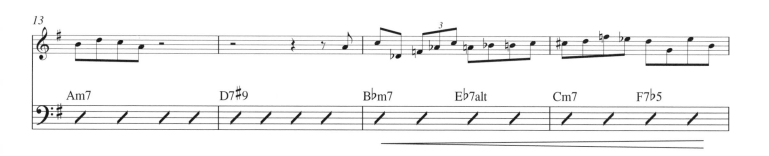

Chords: Am7 | D7♯9 | B♭m7 E♭7alt | Cm7 F7♭5

The Punch Line

(Altered Tone Version)

Realized Version

Medium Swing (♩ = 126)

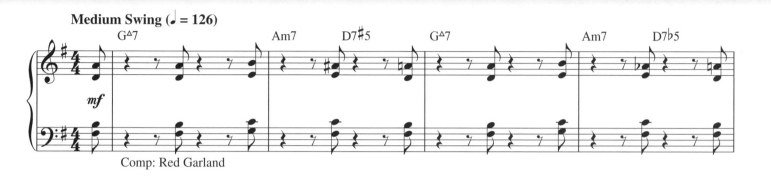

Comp: Red Garland

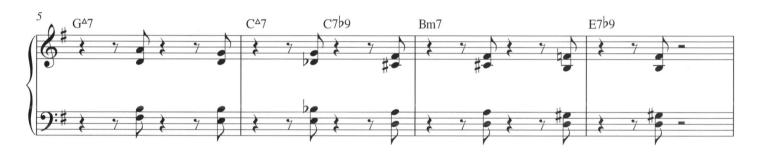

Straight eighths

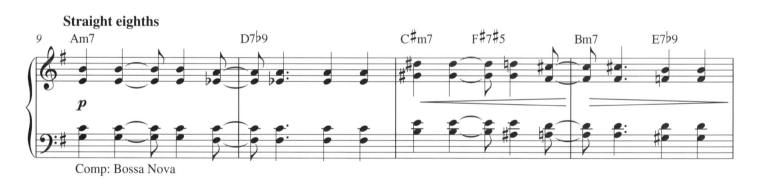

Comp: Bossa Nova

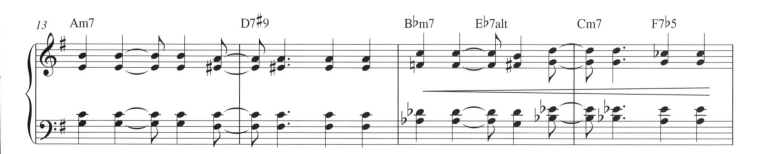

Comp: Red Garland

Dual Identity
Unrealized Version

Hard Swing (♩ = 108)

C7♯9

Comp: Charleston
p

F7♭9

C7♯9

E♭7♯9

F7♯9

E♭7♯9

F7♭5(♭9)

A♭m7   D♭7♭5   A♭m7   D♭7♭5   A♭m7   D♭7♭5   A♭m7   D♭7♭5

Comp: Red Garland
mf

Hard Swing ($\downarrow$ = 108)

Comp: Charleston

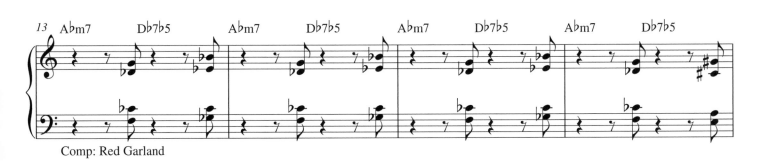

Comp: Red Garland

CHAPTER 12
MINOR ii-V-i's

Thus far, we've only studied ii-V-I's in major keys – that is, where the "I" is a major chord and the other chords are derived from the major scale.

You can also create ii-V-i* progressions in minor keys from the harmonic minor scale. Recall that the harmonic minor scale is like a major scale but with a lowered third and sixth.

C Harmonic Minor

root (i) 2 3 4 5 6 7

Just as with a major ii-V-I, form the chords for a minor ii-V-i by stacking every second note starting from the second, fifth, and root notes of this scale. Since we're now familiar with the ninth, we can create five-note chords:

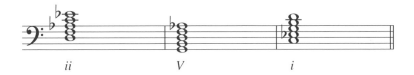

ii V i

The middle chord should look familiar – it's a dominant seventh chord with a flatted ninth. In C minor, the "V" chord is a G7(♭9).

The other two chords are new. The "ii" chord is like a minor seventh chord, but has a flatted fifth and flatted ninth. Any minor seventh chord with a flatted fifth is called a **half-diminished chord**.** There are two ways to write the chord symbol for this chord. One is to call it a minor chord with a flatted fifth – Dm7(♭5). The other is to write a circle with a diagonal slash through it – Dø7. These are equivalent and you should be prepared to read both.

The "i" chord is a kind of hybrid – it has the seventh of a major chord but the third of a minor chord. Because of these qualities, it's called a **minor-major seventh chord** and its symbol is a little "m" followed by a superscript triangle – Cm△7.

* The "i" is now lower case because it represents a minor chord.

** It's called a half-diminished chord regardless of whether the ninth is lowered or not. In fact, for half-diminished chords, you get to choose which kind of ninth you want to use – just make sure your choice doesn't clash with the melody.

Find a ii-V-I progression in E♭ minor.

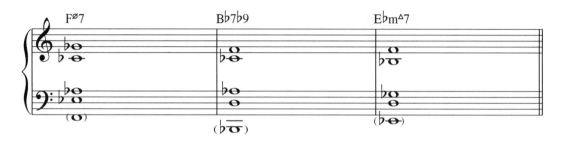

TO THE SHED!

1) **Fill in the Blanks:** Fill in the missing chord symbols to complete these minor ii-V-i progressions.

F⌀7 - _____ - _____

_____ - B7(°9) - _____

D♭°7 - _____ - _____

B♭°7 - _____ - _____

_____ - _____ - Gm△7

_____ - A7(°9) - _____

2) **Name that Chord:** Determine whether the chords below are half-diminished or minor-major seventh. Then write the correct chord symbol above the staff.

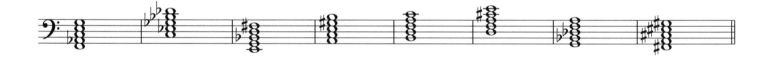

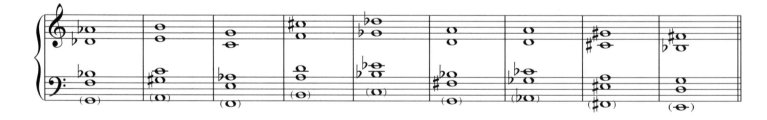

3) **Finish the Job:** Add the necessary flats or sharps to create minor ii-V-i's.

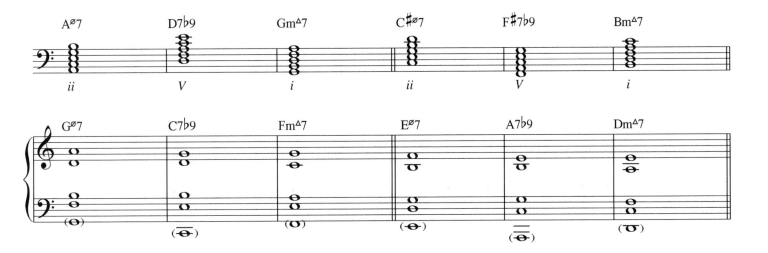

4) **Write it:** Write in the correct chords for the indicated ii-V-i. For the first line, write voicings for the left hand in closed position. For the second line, write the full shell voicing.

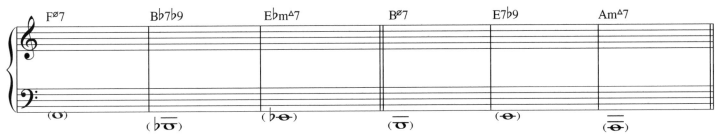

PRACTICING MINOR ii-V-i'S

By this point, you might be able to guess what's coming next: more ii-V-i practice!

Here are some ways to practice minor ii-V-i's:

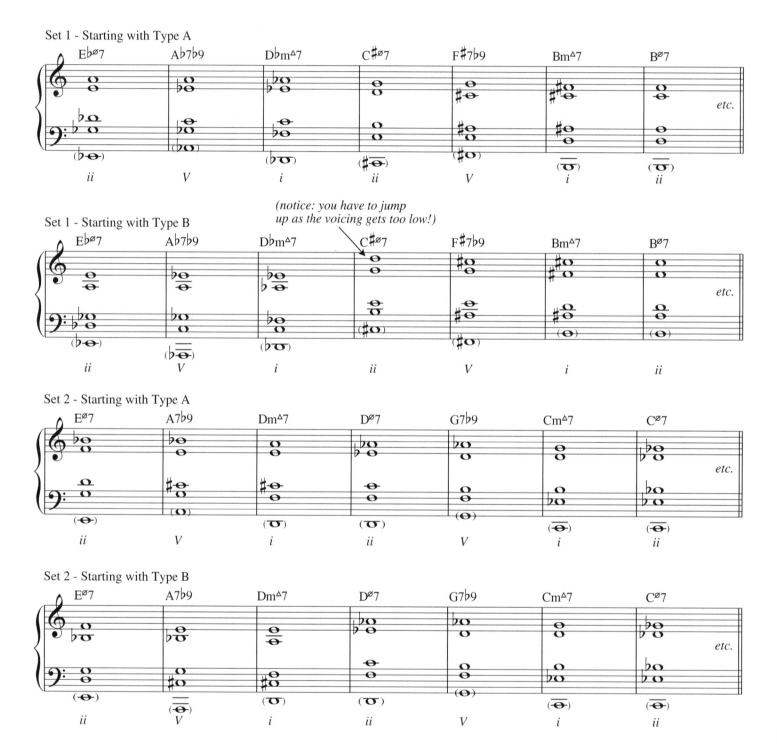

Circle of 5ths - Starting with Type A

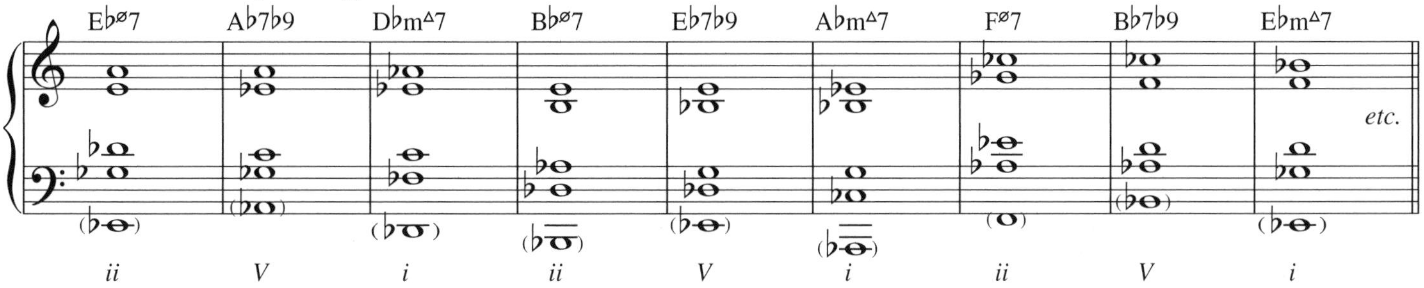

Eᵇø7   Aᵇ7ᵇ9   Dᵇmᐞ7   Bᵇø7   Eᵇ7ᵇ9   Aᵇmᐞ7   Fø7   Bᵇ7ᵇ9   Eᵇmᐞ7

etc.

ii   V   i   ii   V   i   ii   V   i

Circle of 5ths - Starting with Type B

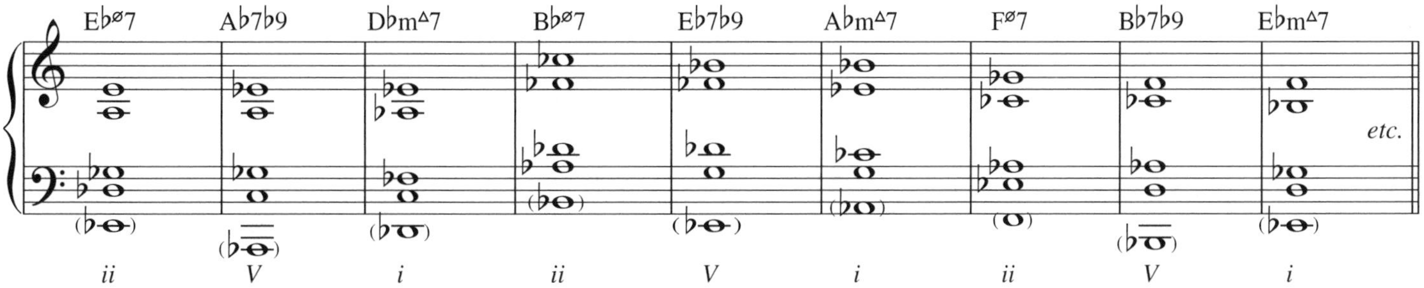

Eᵇø7   Aᵇ7ᵇ9   Dᵇmᐞ7   Bᵇø7   Eᵇ7ᵇ9   Aᵇmᐞ7   Fø7   Bᵇ7ᵇ9   Eᵇmᐞ7

etc.

ii   V   i   ii   V   i   ii   V   i

Chromatic Climb - Starting with Type A

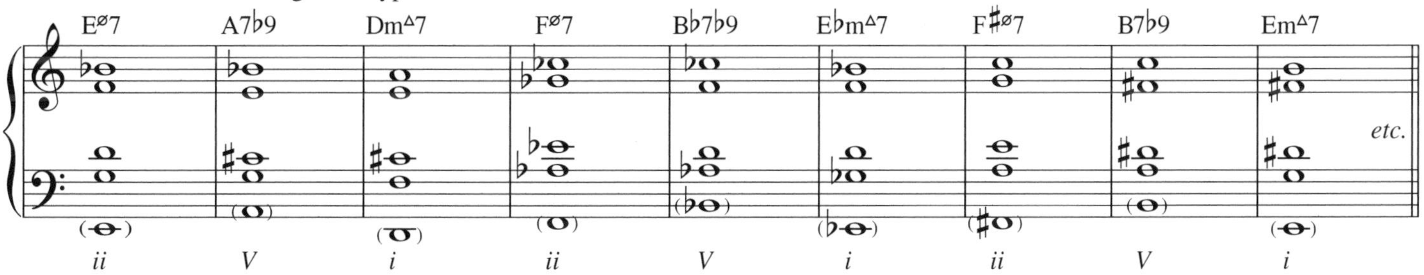

Eø7   A7ᵇ9   Dmᐞ7   Fø7   Bᵇ7ᵇ9   Eᵇmᐞ7   F♯ø7   B7ᵇ9   Emᐞ7

etc.

ii   V   i   ii   V   i   ii   V   i

Chromatic Climb - Starting with Type B

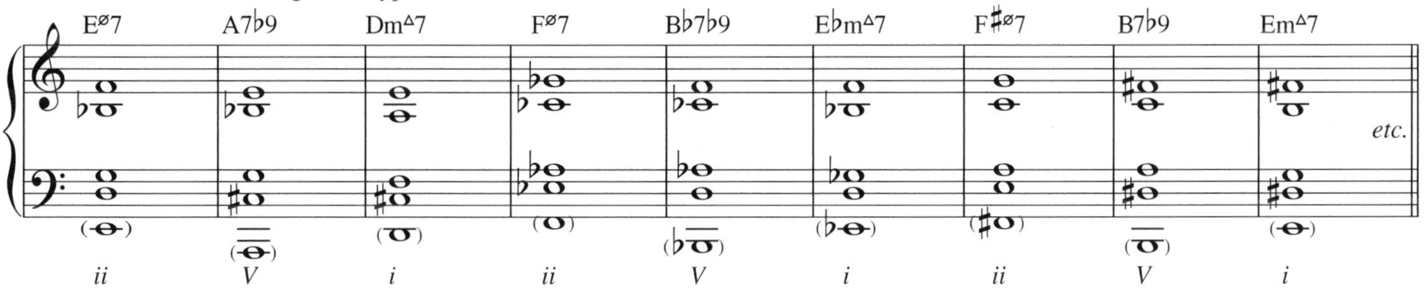

Eø7   A7ᵇ9   Dmᐞ7   Fø7   Bᵇ7ᵇ9   Eᵇmᐞ7   F♯ø7   B7ᵇ9   Emᐞ7

etc.

ii   V   i   ii   V   i   ii   V   i

Bossa Nova (♩ = 104)

Comp: Bossa Nova
mp

p

Cantar
Realized Version

Bossa Nova (♩ = 104)

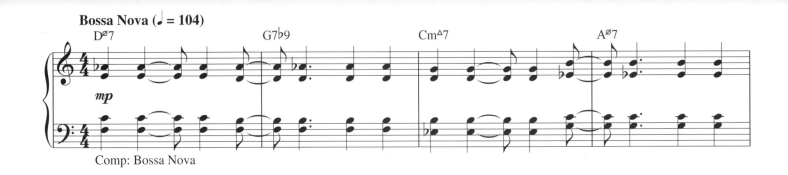

Comp: Bossa Nova

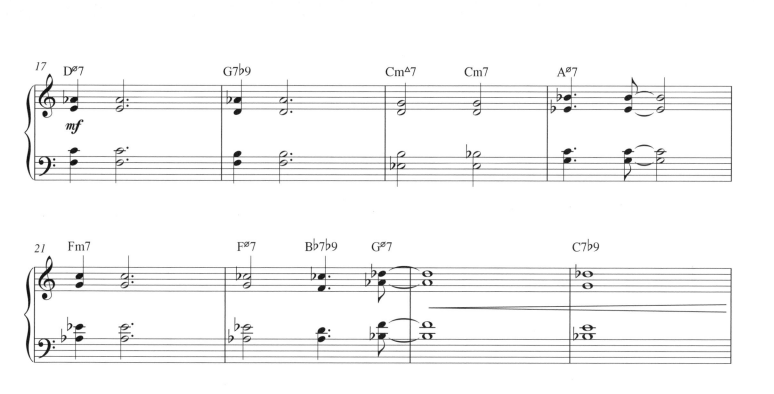

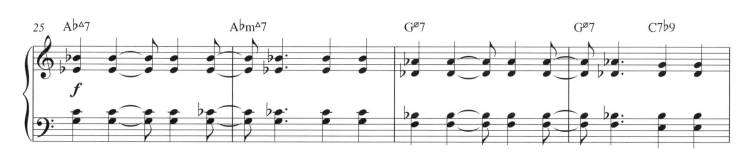

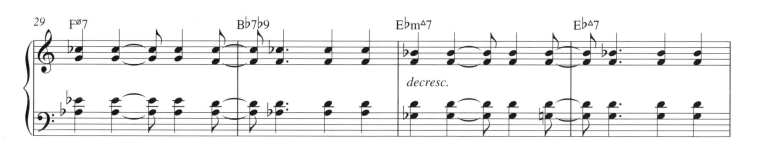

Car Chase

Unrealized Version

Medium fast Swing ($\quarternote = 160$)

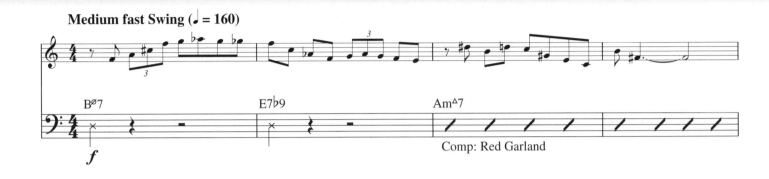

Comp: Red Garland

Medium fast Swing (♩ = 160)

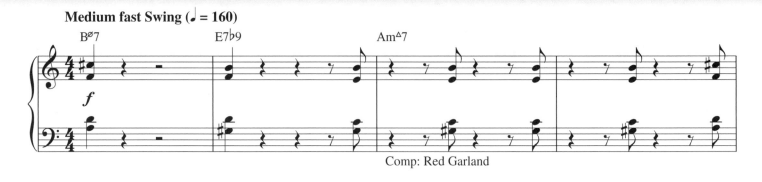

Comp: Red Garland

108

Comp: Charleston

CHAPTER 13

LEFT HAND-ONLY VOICINGS

Because the intervals in shell voicings are large, they require both hands to play. When you need to use your right hand to play the melody or improvise a solo, you can simply play a shell voicing, leaving off the top note.

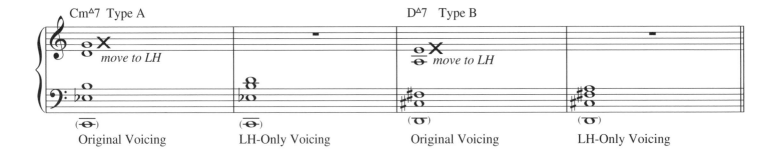

This voicing includes the essential tones – the third and seventh – as well as one color tone – either the fifth (Type B) or the ninth (Type A) – and it fits easily into one hand.

Find left-hand-only voicings for a major ii-V-I in F.

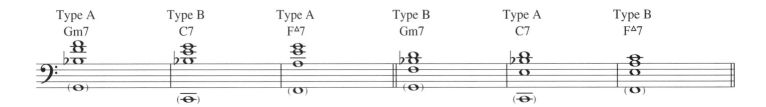

Find left-hand only voicings for a minor ii-V-i in D♭.

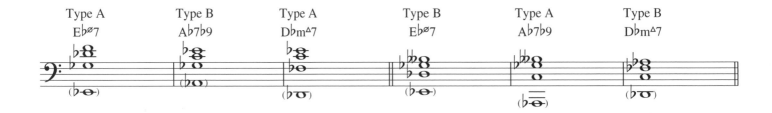

Notice that in the ii-V-i starting with a Type A voicing, there's no fifth for the half-diminished chord, so you can't tell if it's a half-diminished or a regular minor seventh chord. That's okay! You're not required to include all of the tones – so long as you don't play a natural fifth, you're doing fine.

Similarly, in the dominant seventh chord in the next measure, there's no lowered ninth because the Type B voicing includes only the fifth. Once again, this isn't a problem! You're not obligated to include every alteration.

You should practice all your ii-V-I's and ii-V-i's with left hand-only voicings. In addition, practice playing the melodies to some of the pieces in Chapters 11-12 while playing these voicings in the left hand. If you find your hands overlapping, it's perfectly acceptable to raise the melody by an octave to accommodate your left hand.

TO THE SHED!

1) **Change-Up:** Name the chord and write the left hand-only voicing for each chord given.

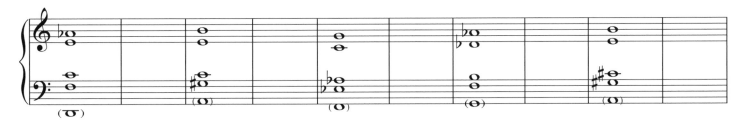

2) **Finish the Job:** Provide the correct accidentals for the following left hand-only ii-V-I progressions.

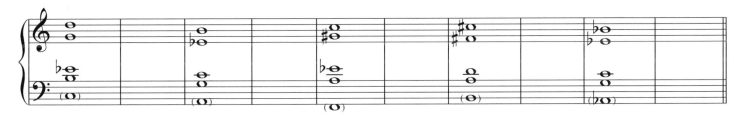

3) **Write It:** Write out the correct left hand-only voicings for the following chords in the position indicated.

Type A

F7b9   Dm△7   Eb△7   Fm7   Ab7#9   Bø7   Am△7   Eb7b5

Type B

Bbm7   Aø7   F#7b5(b9)   C#△7   Abm7   Gm△7   D△7   Gø7   A7#5

CHAPTER 14
UPPER EXTENSIONS & OTHER ALTERATIONS

So far, we've discussed forming chords all the way up to the ninth. If we continue selecting every second note, a chord can be built up to the thirteenth before the notes start repeating. The ninth, eleventh, and thirteenth are collectively known as upper extensions.

Try playing the chord – it doesn't sound very good, right? That's mainly because the chord's eleventh (F) clashes with its third (E). This is commonly fixed by raising the eleventh, creating a C△13(♯11).* This is a very common chord, especially as the final chord of a piece.

Regardless of what chord type you're working with, the upper extensions always come from the major scale unless otherwise indicated. Since the major third also clashes with the eleventh in a dominant thirteenth chord, we must also raise the 11th for this chord:

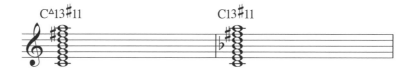

A minor seventh chord, on the other hand, has a lowered third, so there is no conflict between the third and the eleventh. Cm11 or Cm13 chords sound fine with a natural eleventh. Similarly, you can add upper extensions to a Cm△7 chord. However, since the number "7" is necessary in the chord symbol to indicate the major seventh, the extensions are notated using the word "add".

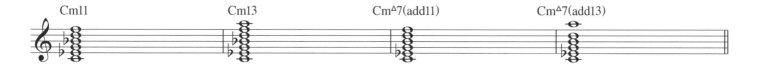

Just because a chord symbol lists the eleventh or thirteenth, it doesn't mean that you're obligated to play that note. Often, the extension reflects a note in the melody and warns you not to play anything that clashes with that note. Conversely, you're permitted to add upper extensions where they're not indicated as long as they don't clash with the rest of the band.

*Upper extensions are indicated in the chord symbol by replacing the "7" with the appropriate extension, like C△13 or B♭m11.

VOICING UPPER EXTENSIONS

When the music indicates an upper extension, you have three choices of how to modify your voicing:

1. You can ignore it.

2. You can add the extension in the right hand of your shell voicing, creating a five-note voicing.

3. You can replace the fifth with the extension indicated.

This third option is the best one to practice – it will add the most variety to your voicings.

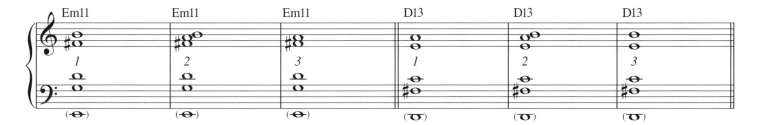

SIXTH CHORDS

Occasionally, a chord symbol will indicate a sixth instead of an odd-numbered extension – as in C6, C△6, or Cm6. These chords are usually used when the root is in the melody to avoid a potential clash between the major seventh and the root.

To voice a "6" chord, replace the chord's seventh with the sixth. Be careful: for all sixth chords, use the sixth from the major scale – that is, two whole steps below the root – do not lower the sixth for minor sixth chords.

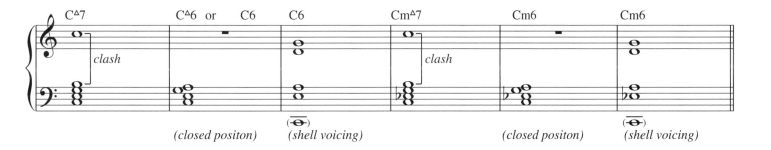

Occasionally, chord symbols like C6/9 or Cm6/9 are used for sixth chords. These indicate the same chords as those above, but they're more specific about the inclusion of the ninth.

ALTERED FIFTHS AND SIXTHS

It's possible to raise the fifth of a major chord and to lower the sixth/thirteenth* of a minor chord. For a major seventh chord with a raised fifth, like G△7(♯5) raise the fifth of a regular shell voicing. For a Gm7(♭6) or Gm7(♭13), replace the seventh with the flatted sixth scale degree or add it next to the seventh to create a five-note voicing.

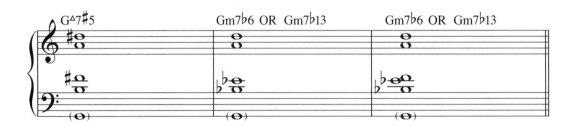

*Think about it: these are the same notes!

TO THE SHED!

1) **Fill-in:** Write the missing extension, either on top or in the middle, to complete the chord.

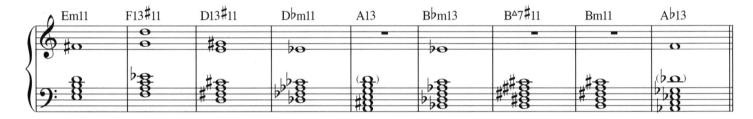

2) **Build It Down:** The note given is the highest extension indicated in the chord symbol. Fill out the rest of the chord based on the evidence provided.

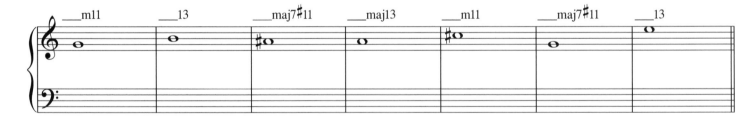

3) **Write it:** Write the missing chord or chord symbol for each measure. Write the chords in shell voicing form

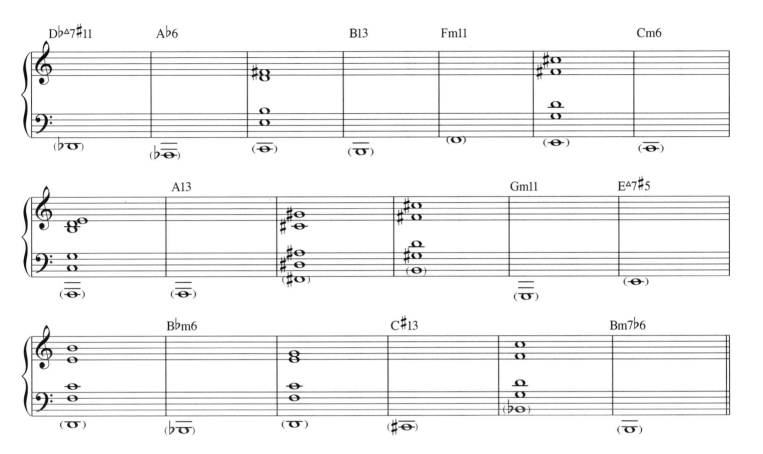

4) **Riddle:** How many years did jazz legend Duke Ellington live? To find out, examine each chord below carefully – one note is incorrect in each chord. Write the number of the incorrect note (1 for the root, 3 for the third, etc.) in the equation below and write the sum.

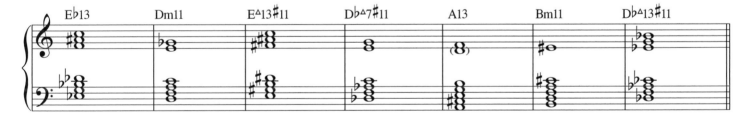

_____ + _____ + _____ + _____ + _____ + _____ + _____ = _____

115

Great Dane
Unrealized Version

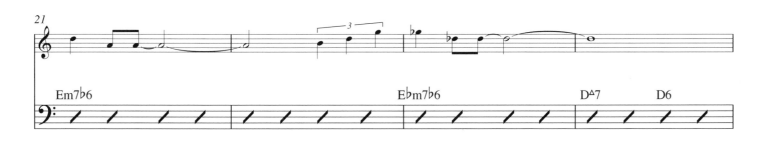

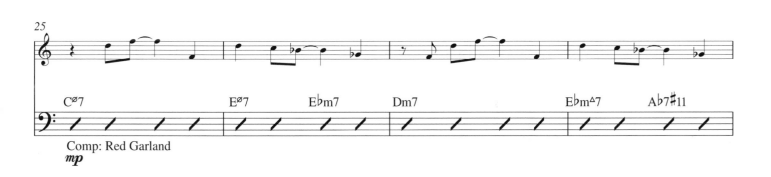

Comp: Red Garland

Great Dane

Realized Version

Realized Version

Medium Swing (♩ = 138)

Comp: Charleston

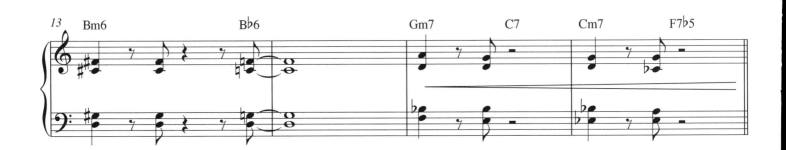

Comp: Red Garland

Misteri
Unrealized Version

Straight eighths (♩ = 108)

Comp: Bossa Nova

Straight eighths ($\quarternote$ = 108)

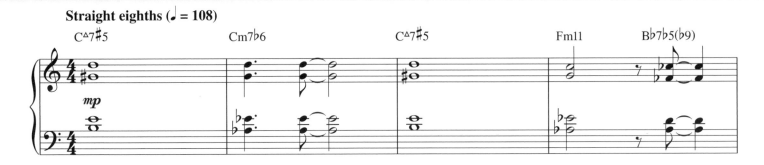

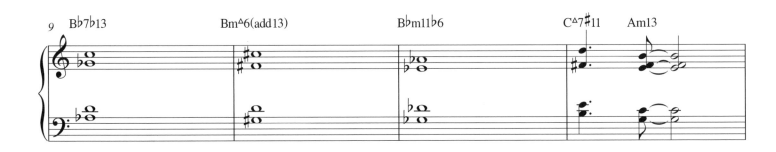

Comp: Bossa Nova

122

Comp: Bossa Nova

CHAPTER 15
OTHER CHORD TYPES & SLASH CHORDS

So far, we've learned five types of jazz chords. Although their altered tones or upper extensions can vary, these chords are our basic harmonic building blocks:

This chapter gives a crash course on four more types of chords and explains inversion notation and voicing for the jazz idiom.

THE DIMINISHED SEVENTH CHORD

A **Diminished Seventh Chord** lowers the third, fifth, and seventh of a dominant seventh chord by a half-step each. The symbol for a diminished seventh chord is a little circle, like the "degree" sign used for temperatures, as in C°7. Diminished seventh chords have a natural ninth and can be voiced with a normal shell voicing:

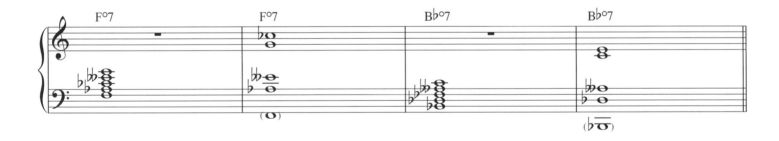

124

THE AUGMENTED CHORD

While the diminished chord has a minor third and a lowered fifth, the **augmented chord** has a major third and a raised fifth. An augmented chord can have either a dominant or major seventh depending on the indication of the chord symbol. If no seventh is indicated, play only a triad. The chord symbol for an augmented chord is a "+" sign.

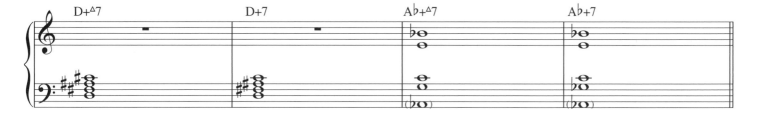

For our purposes, there's no practical difference between an A♭+7 and an A♭7(♯5) or between an A♭7(♯5) and an A♭+△7, but you should be prepared to read either option!

THE SUS/SUS⁴ CHORD

The abbreviation of "**sus**" stands for "suspension." It indicates that the fourth replaces the third, creating suspense as you wait for it to resolve. To hear the traditional function of a "sus" chord, play the progression below:

Sound familiar? This suspension is extremely common in church music and chorales.

To form a "sus" chord, replace the chord's third with the fourth. Like augmented chords, a "sus" chord can have either a lowered or natural seventh depending on the symbol's indication. It's relatively common for "sus" chords to carry lowered ninths – this will always be indicated in the chord symbol.

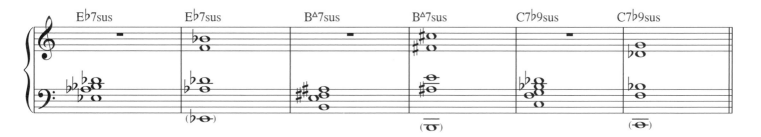

THE "ADD 2" CHORD

This chord symbol indicates a chord with a second/ninth but no seventh. To voice this chord, replace the seventh of a shell voicing with the root. These chords are especially common in pop music.

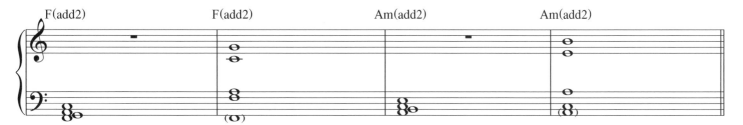

SLASH CHORDS

If you've studied some classical music, you might know that you can **invert** chords – that is, you can reorder the notes, placing a note other than the root at the bottom of the chord. We discussed inversions briefly in Chapter 7 in the context of creating good voice leading.

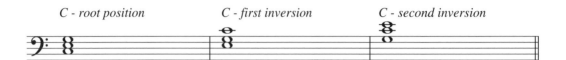

Inversions are also possible in jazz – they are indicated in the chord symbol with a slash, as in Cm7/E♭. This chord symbol is read as "C minor 7 over E♭", or "C minor with an E♭ in the bass".

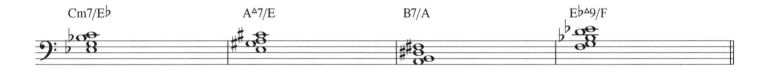

Because the root is no longer played by the bass, it should be added to the piano voicing. For a Type A voicing, add the root above the seventh. For a Type B voicing, add the root between the seventh and the third.

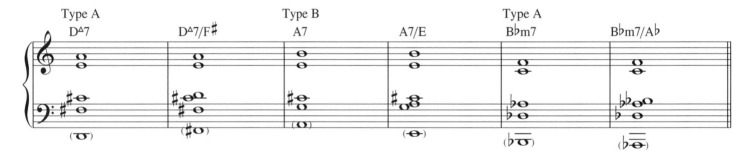

Occasionally, you'll see a slash chord with a bass note that isn't part of the chord. Treat this like an inversion – add the root in the left hand as with other slash chords.

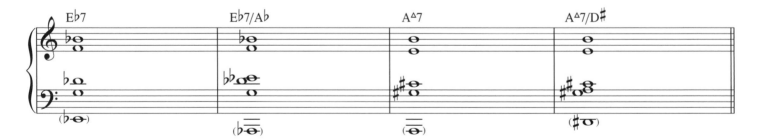

TO THE SHED!

1) **The Name Game:** Write the correct chord symbol for these chords. Keep in mind that some might not have the root in the bass.

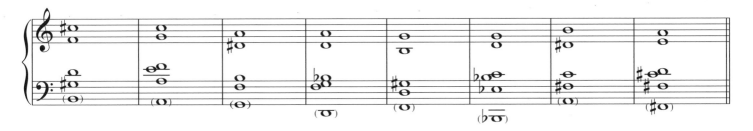

2) **Flip It:** Name the chord for these root position voicings. Then transform them into the inversion with the highlighted note on bottom and name the new chord.

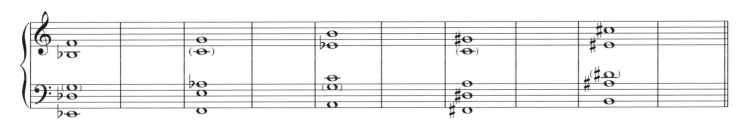

3) **Augmented/Diminished:** Augmented and diminished chords are written out below. Name each chord and write the opposite chord based on the same root note in the next measure. For example, if you see a D augmented chord, write a D diminished chord. This exercise uses major sevenths on all augmented chords.

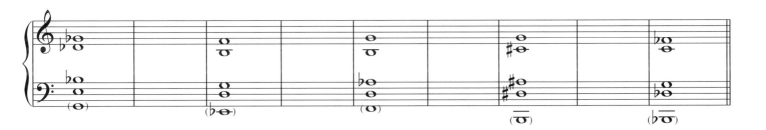

4) **Riddle:** Complete the clues to answer the question: What's really the fastest way to get to Carnegie Hall?

_____   _____   _____   _____

(3rd of a F♯ dim chord)   (5th of a F♭+ chord)   (5th of a D♯dim chord)   (3rd of a G+ chord)

The Cotton Club

Unrealized Version

The Cotton Club
Realized Version

Comp: Red Garland

Dragonfly
Unrealized Version

Dragonfly
Realized Version

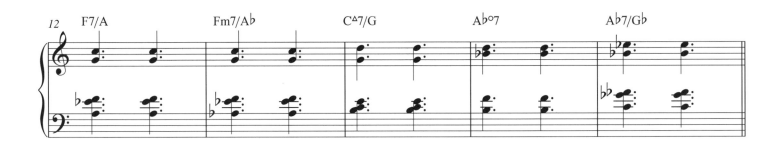

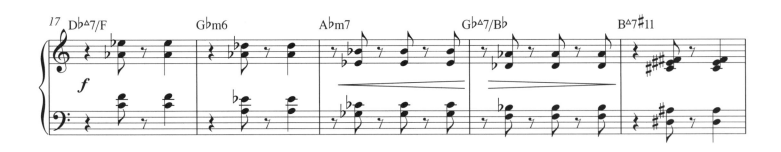

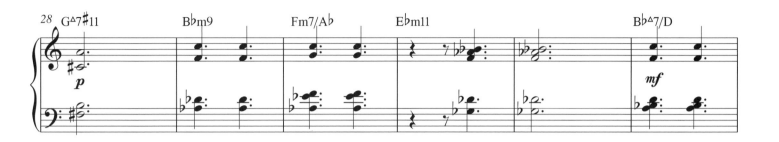

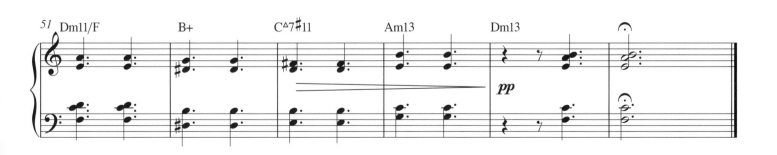

The Fates
Unrealized Version

The Fates
Realized Version

Medium fast Swing (♩ = 168)

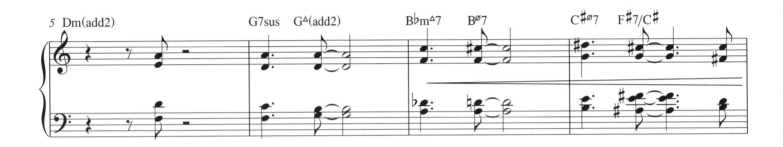

APPENDIX

ANSWERS TO "TO THE SHED" QUESTIONS
CHAPTER 2 – MAJOR TRIADS

1) Complete the Chord: 1. A; 2. F; 3. C#; 4. G#; 5. D#; 6. B; 7. G; 8. C; 9. F#

2) Mismatch: 1. A♭; 2. B♭; 3. D♭ (B♭ does not fit; E♭ would be a better fit)
               4. C; 5. E; 6. A (C does not fit; D would be a better fit)
               7. B♭; 8. B, 9. D♭ (D♭ does not fit; G♭ would be a better fit)

3) Sudoku: Top left: F, top middle: B♭, middle left: D, bottom right: G

4) Chords/Melodies: 1. E♭; 2. A♭; 3. B♭; 4. F; 5. D; 6. C; 7. C#; 8. F#

CHAPTER 3 – MAJOR SEVENTH CHORDS

1) Grouping: (First Group) 1. D♭△7, 2. E♭△7, 3. A♭△7
               (Second Group) 1. D△7, 2. E△7, 3. A△7
               (Third Group) 1. G△7, 2. B♭△7
               (Fourth Group) 1. G♭△7, 2. B△7

2) Complete the Chord: 1. F# & A; 2. B & D; 3. G# & B; 4. C & E♭; 5. F & A♭; 6. D & F; 7. A & C; 8. C# & E;
9. B♭ & D♭; 10. E♭ & G♭

3) Mismatch: 1. The fourth chord does not belong (the top note should be E natural); 2. The second chord does
not belong (the A should be an A#)

CHAPTER 4 – DOMINANT SEVENTH CHORDS

1) Fill-in:

140

2) Mixer:

3) Riddles: A) C♭△7 and C7; B) E7, C7, A7, F♯7

4) Grouping:

Dominant 7th chords on all white keys (one)	G7
Dominant 7th chords with only one black key (five)	C7, D7, E7, F7, A7
Dominant 7th chords with two black keys (three)	D♭7, B♭7, B7
Dominant 7th chords with three black keys (three)	E♭7, G♭7, A♭7

CHAPTER 5 – MINOR TRIADS

1) Word search:

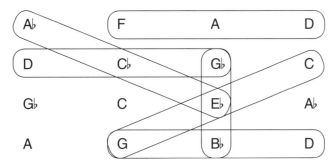

2) Major Chord, Minor Chord: 1. A♭, Dm; minor chord is second; 2. F, D♭m; minor chord is second;
3. D, Cm; minor chord is second; 4. B♭m, E; minor chord is first; 5. Am, G♭; minor chord is first

3) Mixer:

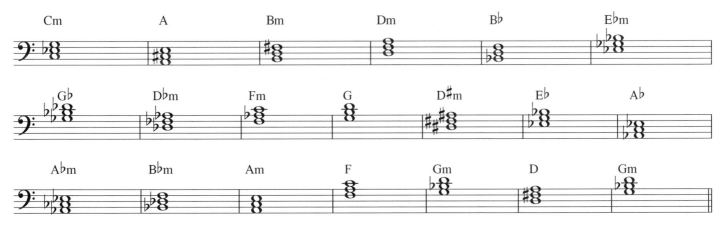

4) Riddle: A   B-E-E

CHAPTER 6 – MINOR SEVENTH CHORDS

1) Complete the Chord: 1. D; 2. G♭; 3. B♭; 4. A; 5. E♭; 6. A♭; 7. F; 8. C; 9. E♭; 10. B; 11. D; 12. A♯; 13. G; 14. A; 15. E♭; 16. F

2) Scramble: 1. Fm7; 2. Am7; 3. F♯m7; 4. Bm7; 5. B♭m7; 6. Cm7

3) Fill-in:

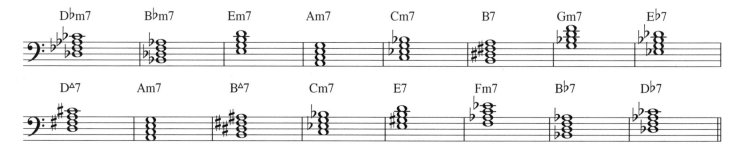

4) Riddle: A) Fm7; B) Dm7; C) E♭△7; D) B7; E) A♭m or "A flat miner"

CHAPTER 7 – THE II-V-I PROGRESSION

1) Fill-in: 1. D, A7; 2. B♭; 3. G♭; 4. A△7; 5. F♯7; 6. D♯m7, C♯△7

2) Missing Pieces:

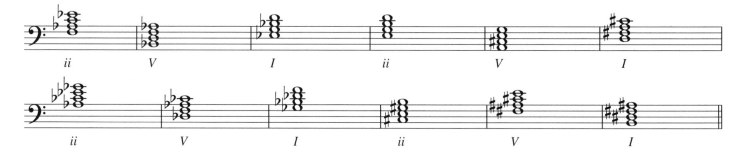

3) Search Committee:

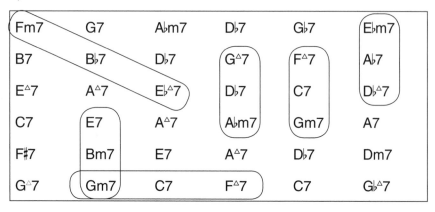

CHAPTER 9 – THE 9TH

1) What Doesn't Belong: 1. The 3rd chord (G△7); 2. The last chord (C♯m9); 3. The last chord (F9)

2) Fill-in: 1. B♭; 2. C♯; 3. A; 4. D♯; 5. F♯; 6. C; 7. G; 8. E♯; 9. C♯; 10. G; 11. E♯; 12. C♯; 13. G; 14. C; 15. E; 16. B

3) Yes. Even if the chord symbol doesn't specify a ninth, it is perfectly acceptable to use the ninth

4) BEET

CHAPTER 10 – SHELL VOICINGS

1) A or B: 1. A; 2. B; 3. B; 4. B; 5. B; 6. A; 7. B; 8. B; 9. B; 10. A; 11. B; 12. A; 13. B; 14. B; 15. A

2) Transformations:

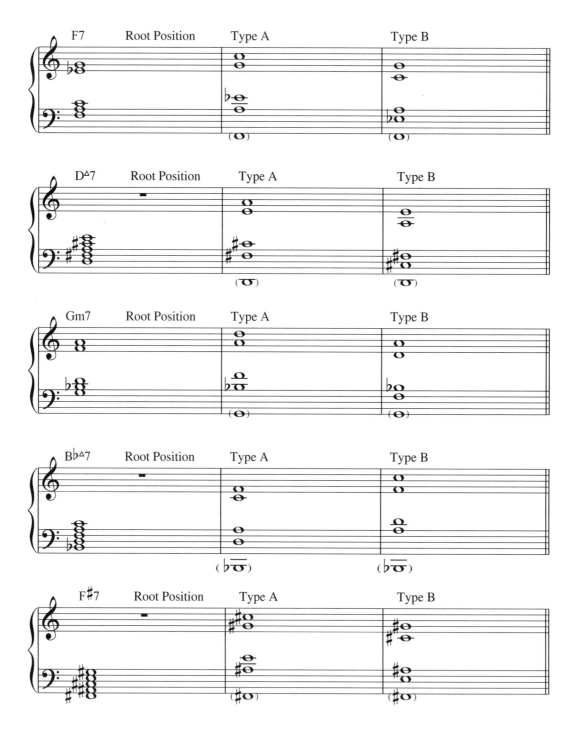

3) Fill-in:

CHAPTER 11 – ALTERED TONES

1) Finish the Job: 1. ♭5; 2. ♭5, ♭9; 3. ♯5; 4. ♯5, ♯9; 5. ♯9; 6. ♯5; 7. ♯5, ♯9; 8. ♭9; 9. ♭9; 10. ♯5, ♯9; 11. ♯9; 12. (none); 13. ♭5; 14. ♯5, ♭9

2) Allowed or Forbidden: 1. Forbidden (C conflicts with ♯5); 2. Allowed; 3. Forbidden (D clashes with altered 9); 4. Allowed; 5. Forbidden (F clashes with flat 5); 6. Forbidden (A♭ clashes with flat 5)

3) Write it Out:

CHAPTER 12 – MINOR ii-V-i'S

1) Fill in the Blanks: 1. B♭7(♭9), E♭m△7; 2. F♯7, Em△7; 3. G♭7(♭9)-C♭m△7; 4. E♭7(♭9), A♭m△7; 5. A⌀7, D7(♭9); 6. E⌀7, Dm△7

2) Name that Chord: 1. Fm△7; 2. C⌀7; 3. E⌀7; 4. Am△7; 5. B⌀7; 6. Dm△7; 7. G⌀7; 8. F♯m△7; 9. G⌀7; 10. Am△7; 11. Fm△7; 12. B⌀7; 13. C⌀7; 14. Gm△7; 13. A♭⌀7; 14. F♯m△7; 15. E⌀7

3) Finish the Job: 1. E, optional B♭; 2. F♯, E♭; 3. B♭, F♯; 4. C♯, optional D♯; 5. F♯, A♯, C♯; 6. F♯, A♯, C♯; 7. B♭, D♭, optional A♭; 8. B♭, D♭; 9. A♭, 10. B♭, optional F♯; 11. C♯, B♭; 12. C♯

4) Write it:

CHAPTER 13 – LEFT HAND-ONLY VOICINGS

1) Change-Up:

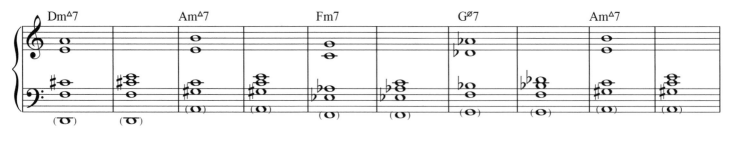

2) Finish the Job: measure 1. A♭, E♭; 2. A♭; 3. <none>; 4. <optional D♯>; 5. A♯; C♯; 6. A♯, C♯; 7. <none>; 8. F♯; 9. F♯; 10. <none>; 11. D♯; 12. D♯; 13. G♭, D♭; 14. G♭, E♭; 15. E♭; 16. <none>; 17. G♯; 18. G♯

Write It:

Type A

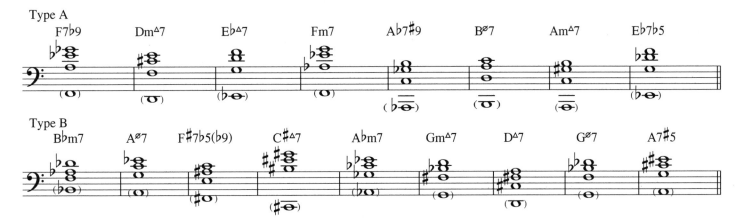

CHAPTER 14 – UPPER EXTENSIONS & OTHER ALTERATIONS

1) Fill-in: 1. A; 2. B; 3. B; 4. G♭; 5. F♯; 6. G; 7. E♯; 8. E; 9. B♭

2) Build Downwards: 1. Dm11 (from top: G-E-C-A-F-D); 2. D13 (B-(G)-E-C-A-F♯-D); 3. E△7(♯11) (A♯-F♯-D♯-B-G♯-E)
4. Cmaj13 (A-(F)-D-B-G-E-C); 5. G♯m11 (C♯-A♯-F♯-D♯-B-G♯) 6. D♭△7(♯11) (G-E♭-C-A♭-F-D♭); 7. G13 (E-(C)-A-F-D-B-G)

3) Write it:

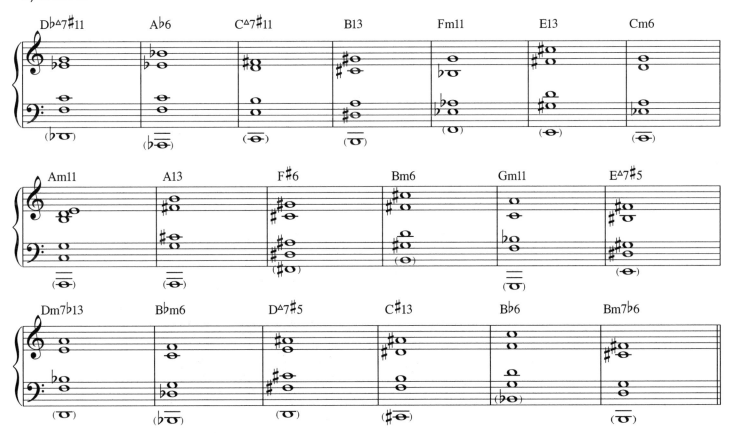

4) Riddle: 11 + 11 + 13 + 9 + 13 + 11 + 7 = 75. He lived 75 years.

CHAPTER 15 – OTHER CHORD TYPES & SLASH CHORDS

1) The Name Game: 1. E♭△7/G; 2. G#°7; 3. B♭△7(#5) or B♭+△7 4. Esus7; 5. C#°7; 6. F#△7/C#; 7. A7/C#; 8. D#°7; 9. Gm7/B♭; 10. B°7; 11. F△7/A; 12. G+7 or G7(#5) 13. Gm7/D; 14. F°7; 15. Cm7/B♭; 16. A°7; 17. D△7/F#

2) Flip it:

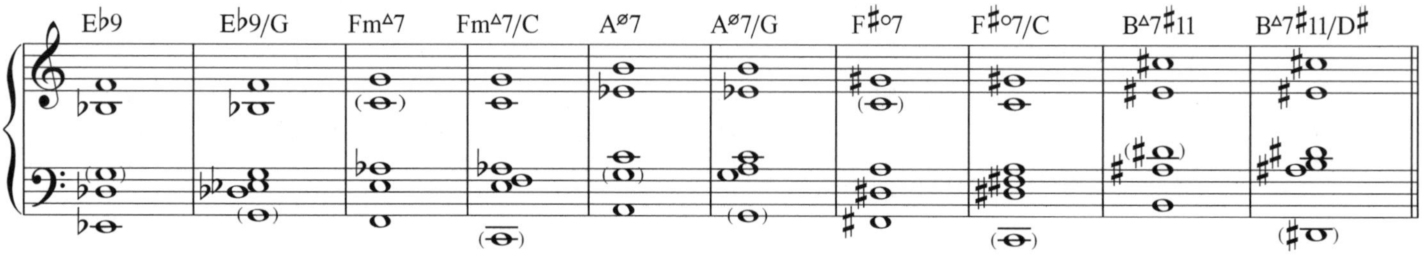

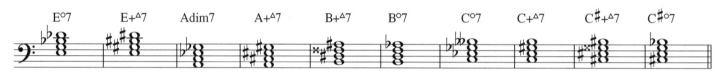

3)

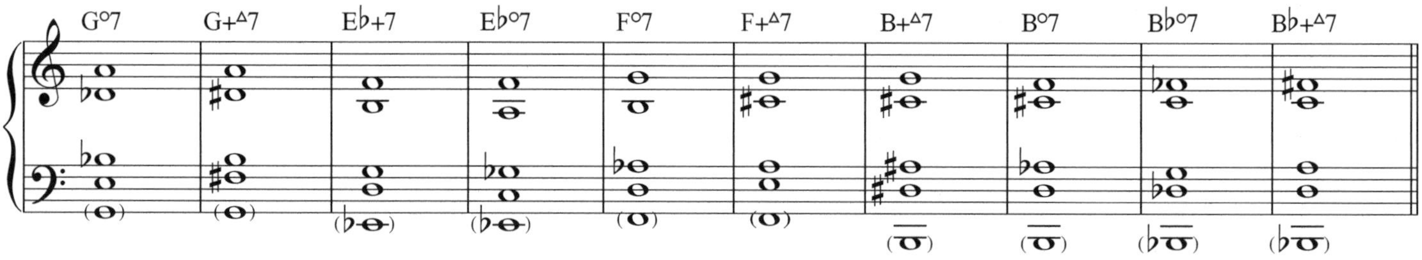

4) A CAB

FULL ii–V–I SEQUENCES
METAMORPHOSIS – SET I

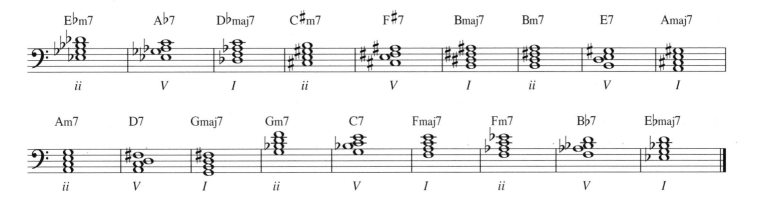

METAMORPHOSIS – SET II

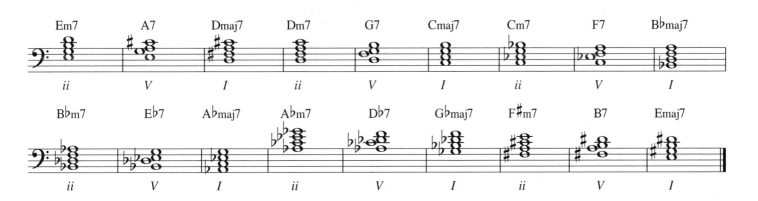

CIRCLE OF FIFTHS

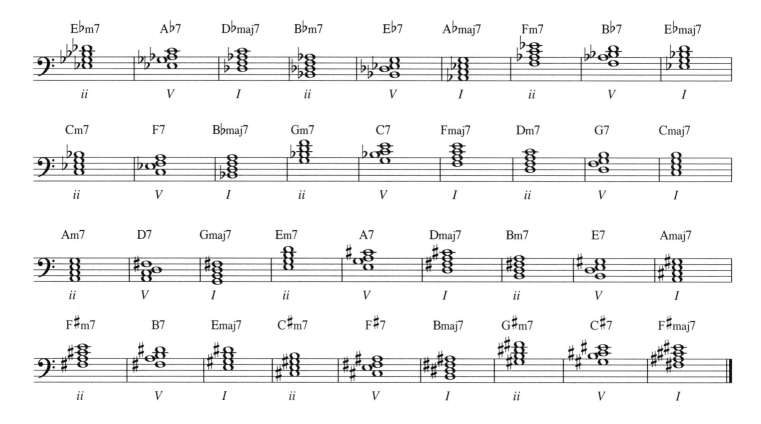

CHROMATIC CLIMB

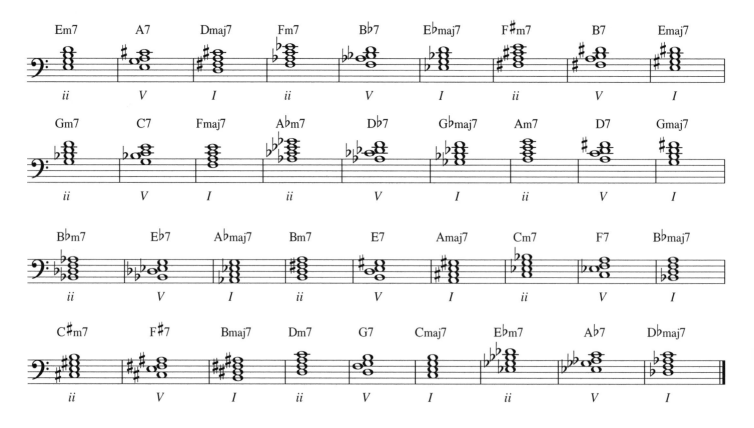

20 GREAT JAZZ ALBUMS FEATURING
20 GREAT PIANISTS

(in no particular order)

1. *Night Train* – Oscar Peterson Trio

2. *Sunday at the Village Vanguard* – Bill Evans Trio

3. *'Round Midnight* – Miles Davis (pianist Red Garland)

4. *Blues in Orbit* – Duke Ellington

5. *Chairman of the Board* – Count Basie and his Orchestra

6. *Smokin' at the Half Note* – Wes Montgomery (pianist Wynton Kelly)

7. *Blue Train* – John Coltrane (pianist Kenny Drew)

8. *Moanin'* – Art Blakey and the Jazz Messengers (pianist Bobby Timmons)

9. *Criss-Cross* – Thelonious Monk

10. *At the Pershing* – Ahmad Jamal

11. *The Amazing Bud Powell* – Bud Powell

12. *Somethin' Else* – Cannonball Adderley (pianist Hank Jones)

13. *Takin' Off* – Herbie Hancock

14. *Jazz Moments* – George Shearing

15. *Tenor Madness* – Sonny Rollins (pianist Tommy Flanagan)

16. *A World of Piano* – Phineas Newborn, Jr.

17. *The Cape Verdean Blues* – Horace Silver

18. *Cool Struttin'* – Sonny Clark

19. *Concert by the Sea* – Erroll Garner

20. *Doin' Alright* – Dexter Gordon (pianist Horace Parlan)

Expand Your Jazz Piano Technique

BLUES, JAZZ & ROCK RIFFS FOR KEYBOARDS
by William T. Eveleth
Because so much of today's popular music has its roots in blues, the material included here is a vital component of jazz, rock, R&B, gospel, soul, and even pop. The author has compiled actual licks, riffs, turnaround phrases, embellishments, and basic patterns that define good piano blues and can be used as a basis for players to explore and create their own style.
00221028 Book..........................$9.95

BOOGIE WOOGIE FOR BEGINNERS
by Frank Paparelli
This bestseller is now available with a CD of demonstration tracks! A short easy method for learning to play boogie woogie, designed for the beginner and average pianist. Includes: exercises for developing left-hand bass; 25 popular boogie woogie bass patterns; arrangements of "Down the Road a Piece" and "Answer to the Prayer" by well-known pianists; a glossary of musical terms for dynamics, tempo and style; and more.
00312559 Book/CD Pack $14.99

A CLASSICAL APPROACH TO JAZZ PIANO IMPROVISATION
by Dominic Alldis
This keyboard instruction book is designed for the person who was trained classically but wants to expand into the very exciting — yet very different — world of jazz improvisation. Author Dominic Alldis provides clear explanations and musical examples of: pentatonic improvisation; the blues; rock piano; rhythmic placement; scale theory; major, minor and pentatonic scale theory applications; and more.
00310979 Book.................. $16.95

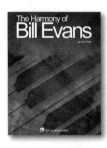

THE HARMONY OF BILL EVANS
by Jack Reilly
A compilation of articles — now revised and expanded — that originally appeared in the quarterly newsletter *Letter from Evans*, this unique folio features extensive analysis of Evans' work. Pieces examined include: B Minor Waltz • Funny Man • How Deep Is the Ocean • I Fall in Love Too Easily • I Should Care • Peri's Scope • Time Remembered • and Twelve Tone Tune.
00699405 Book.................$19.99

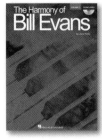

THE HARMONY OF BILL EVANS - VOLUME 2
by Jack Reilly
Reilly's second volume includes two important theory chapters, plus ten of Bill's most passionate and melodically gorgeous works. The accompanying audio CD will add to the enjoyment, understanding, and appreciation of the written examples. Songs include: For Nenette • January • Laurie • Maxine • Song for Helen • Turn Out the Stars • Very Early • Waltz for Debby • and more.
00311828 Book/CD Pack $29.99

AN INTRODUCTION TO JAZZ CHORD VOICING FOR KEYBOARD - 2ND EDITION
by Bill Boyd
This book is designed for the pianist/keyboardist with moderate technical skills and reading ability who desires to play jazz styles and learn to improvise from reading chord symbols. It is an ideal self-teaching book for keyboardists in high school and junior high jazz ensembles. Unique features of this book include chords and progressions written out in all keys, a simple fingering system which applies to all keys, and coverage of improvising and solo playing.
00854100 Book/CD Pack................$19.95

INTROS, ENDINGS & TURNAROUNDS FOR KEYBOARD
ESSENTIAL PHRASES FOR SWING, LATIN, JAZZ WALTZ, AND BLUES STYLES
by John Valerio
Learn the intros, endings and turnarounds that all of the pros know and use! This new keyboard instruction book by John Valerio covers swing styles, ballads, Latin tunes, jazz waltzes, blues, major and minor keys, vamps and pedal tones, and more.
00290525 Book $12.95

JAZZ ETUDE INSPIRATIONS
EIGHT PIANO ETUDES INSPIRED BY THE MASTERS
by Jeremy Siskind
Etudes in the style of legendary greats Oscar Peterson, Duke Ellington, McCoy Tyner, Jelly Roll Morton, Chick Corea, Brad Mehldau, Count Basie and Herbie Hancock will help students master some technical challenges posed by each artist's individual style. The performance notes include a biography, practice tips and a list of significant recordings. Tunes include: Count on Me • Hand Battle • Jelly Roll Me Home • Minor Tyner • Oscar's Bounce • Pineapple Woman • Repeat After Me • Tears Falling on Still Water.
00296860 Book........................$8.99

JAZZ PIANO
by Liam Noble
Featuring lessons, music, historical analysis and rare photos, this book/CD pack provides a complete overview of the techniques and styles popularized by 15 of the greatest jazz pianists of all time. All the best are here: from the early ragtime stylings of Ferdinand "Jelly Roll" Morton, to the modal escapades of Bill Evans, through the '70s jazz funk of Herbie Hancock. CD contains 15 full-band tracks.
00311050 Book/CD Pack $17.95

JAZZ PIANO CONCEPTS & TECHNIQUES
by John Valerio
This book provides a step-by-step approach to learning basic piano realizations of jazz and pop tunes from lead sheets. Systems for voicing chords are presented from the most elementary to the advanced along with methods for practicing each system. Both the non-jazz and the advanced jazz player will benefit from the focus on: chords, chord voicings, harmony, melody and accompaniment, and styles.
00290490 Book $16.95

JAZZ PIANO TECHNIQUE
by John Valerio
This one-of-a-kind book applies traditional technique exercises to specific jazz piano needs. Topics include: scales (major, minor, chromatic, pentatonic, etc.), arpeggios (triads, seventh chords, upper structures), finger independence exercises (static position, held notes, Hanon exercises), and more! The CD includes 45 recorded examples.
00312059 Book/CD Pack................$19.99

JAZZ PIANO VOICINGS
by Rob Mullins
Long-time performer and educator Rob Mullins helps players enter the jazz world by providing voicings that will help the player develop skills in the jazz genre and start sounding professional right away — without years of study! Includes a "Numeric Voicing Chart," chord indexes in all 12 keys, info about what range of the instrument you can play chords in, and a beginning approach to bass lines.
00310914 Book........................$19.95

Prices, contents, and availability subject to change without notice.

HAL•LEONARD®
CORPORATION
7777 W. BLUEMOUND RD. P.O. BOX 13819 MILWAUKEE, WI 53213
www.halleonard.com

1213